Nozomu Tamaki Presents Dance In The Vampire Bund 1

DANCE IN THE VAMPIRE BUND

1

NOZOMU TAMAKI

Sein Reich komme!

Nichts ist wirklicher als diese Illusion.

Sie hat die Dome erbaut,

sie hat die Dome zertrümmert,

Jahrtausende haben gesungen,

gelitten,

gemordet für dieses Reich,

das niemals kommt

—und dennoch ......ze menschliche Geschichte!

......come!

...... this illusion.

...... cathedrals.

...... have sung, suffered and murdered one another

For this illusive kingdom that never comes.

—And so it is responsible for the whole of human history.

Frisch "Nun singen sie wieder"

Dance In The Vampire Bund 1

Contents

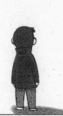

ONCE UPON A TIME, A YOUNG BOY ASKED THE QUEEN OF THE MONSTERS A QUESTION...

"YOU'RE ALWAYS STARING SADLY OUT AT THE WORLD. HOW LONG ARE YOU GOING TO KEEP DOING THAT?"

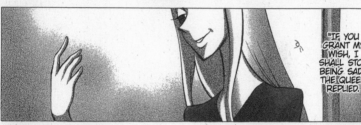

"IF YOU GRANT MY WISH, I SHALL STOP BEING SAD," THE QUEEN REPLIED.

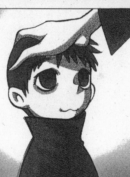

"I WILL," THE BOY NODDED VIGOROUSLY.

"BUT IF YOU BREAK YOUR WORD...I SHALL *EAT* YOU. SO, DEAR BOY, WILL YOU STILL MAKE YOUR PROMISE?"

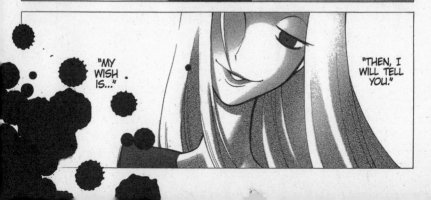

"MY WISH IS..."

"THEN, I WILL TELL YOU."

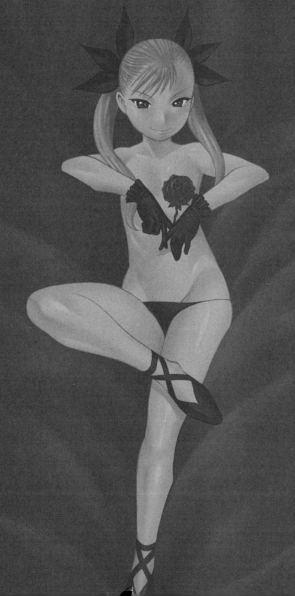

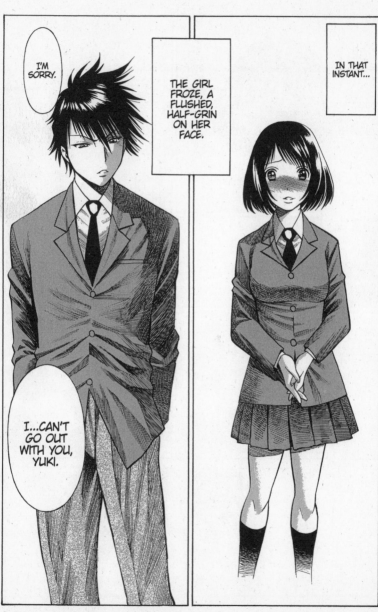

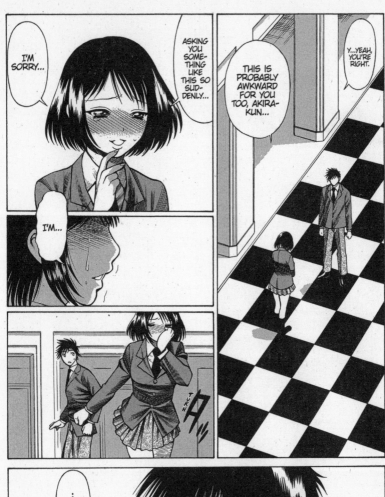

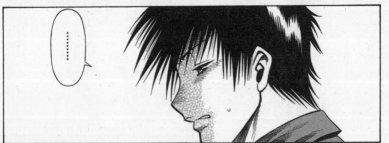

6

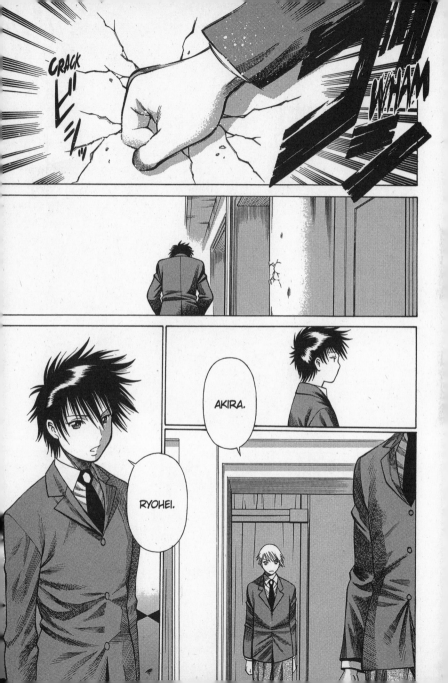

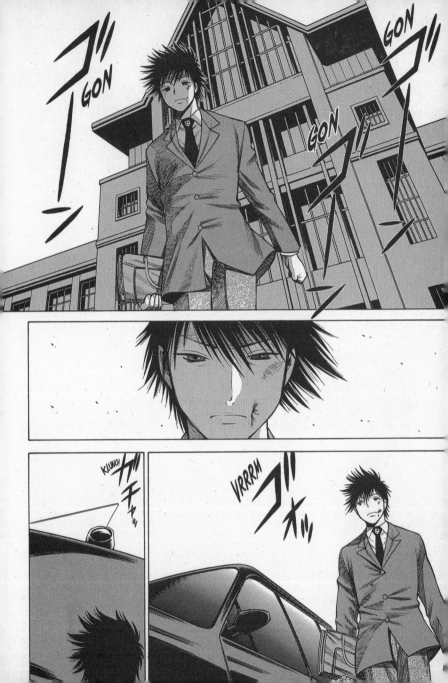

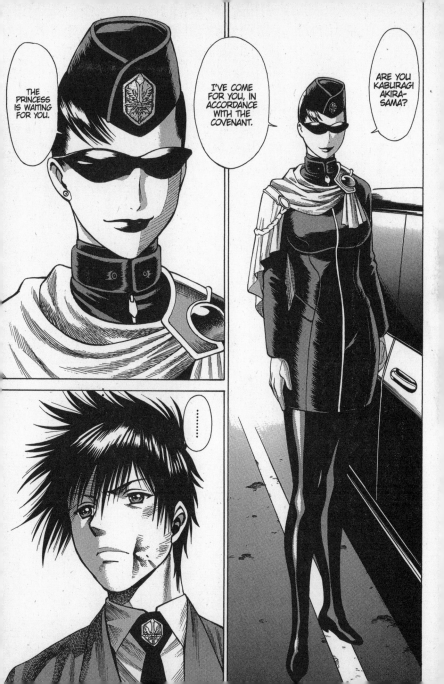

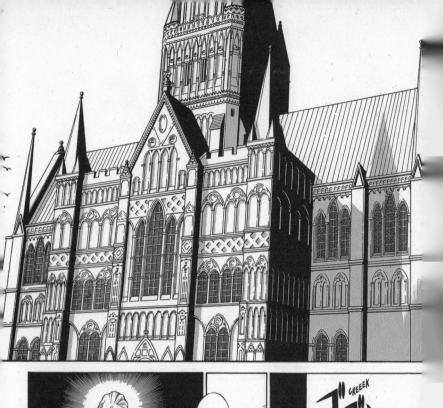

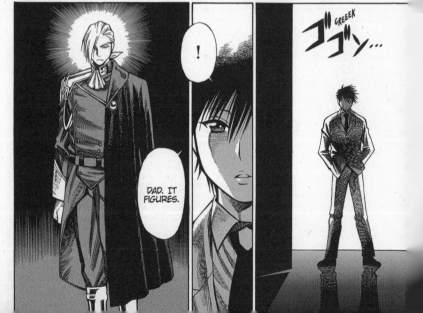

ゴ゙゙ GREEEK
ゴ゙ゴン...

！

DAD. IT
FIGURES.

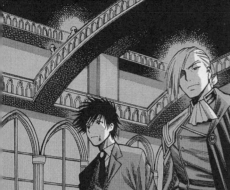

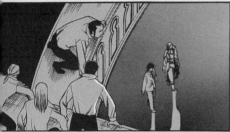

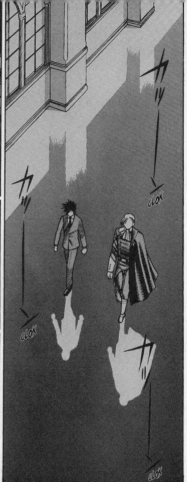

NOTH-ING.

WHAT HAPPENED TO YOUR FACE?

IT'LL HEAL IN NO TIME.

WHY? I'M NOT HUMAN.

USE THIS.

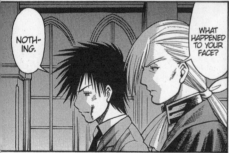

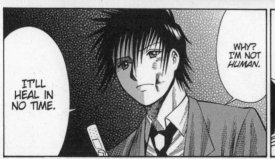

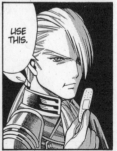

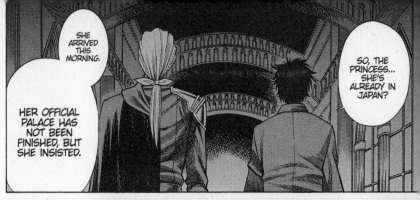

SHE ARRIVED THIS MORNING.

HER OFFICIAL PALACE HAS NOT BEEN FINISHED, BUT SHE INSISTED.

SO, THE PRINCESS... SHE'S ALREADY IN JAPAN?

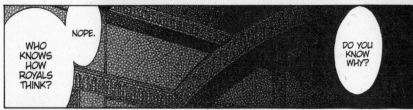

NOPE.

WHO KNOWS HOW ROYALS THINK?

DO YOU KNOW WHY?

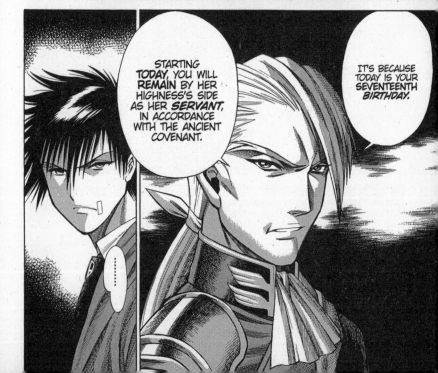

STARTING TODAY, YOU WILL REMAIN BY HER HIGHNESS'S SIDE AS HER *SERVANT*, IN ACCORDANCE WITH THE ANCIENT COVENANT.

IT'S BECAUSE TODAY IS YOUR SEVENTEENTH *BIRTHDAY*.

....

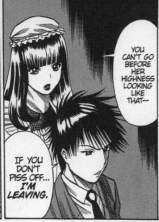

YOU CAN'T GO BEFORE HER HIGHNESS LOOKING LIKE THAT—

IF YOU DON'T PISS OFF... I'M LEAVING.

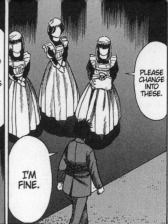

PLEASE CHANGE INTO THESE.

I'M FINE.

YOU'RE RIGHT.

THIS *IS* MORE MY STYLE.

THANKS.

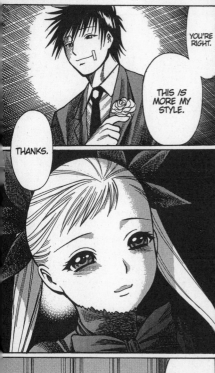

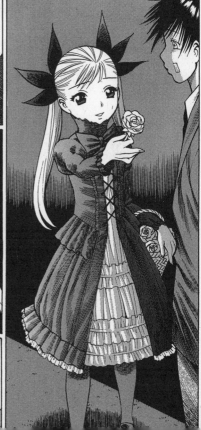

HER HIGHNESS IS WAITING.

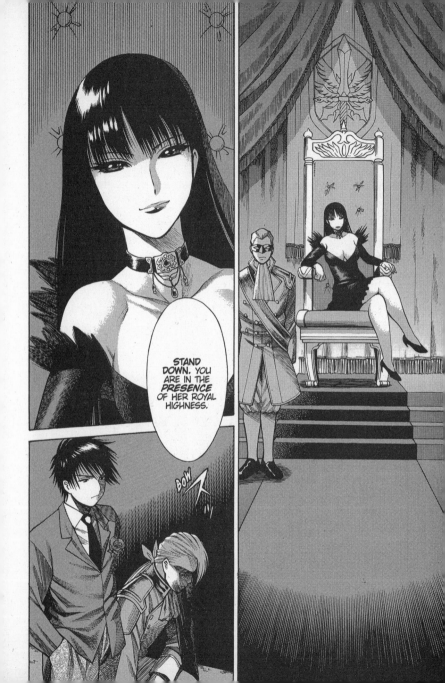

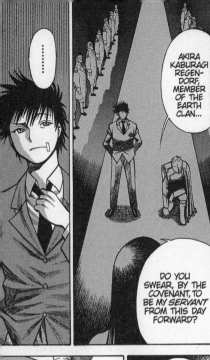

· · · · · · · · · ·

AKIRA KABURAGI REGEN-DORF, MEMBER OF THE EARTH CLAN...

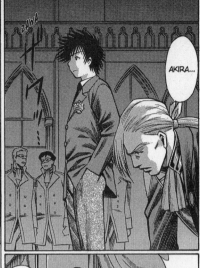

AKIRA...

DO YOU SWEAR, BY THE COVENANT, TO BE MY *SERVANT* FROM THIS DAY FORWARD?

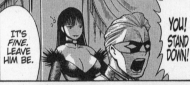

IT'S *FINE*. LEAVE HIM BE.

YOU! STAND DOWN!

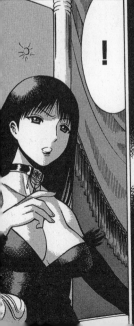

!

HELL NO.

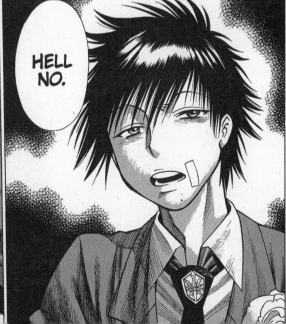

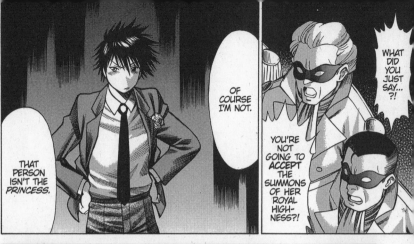

OF COURSE I'M NOT.

WHAT DID YOU JUST SAY...?!

YOU'RE NOT GOING TO ACCEPT THE SUMMONS OF HER ROYAL HIGHNESS?!

THAT PERSON ISN'T THE *PRINCESS*.

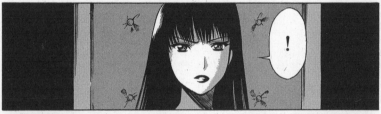

!

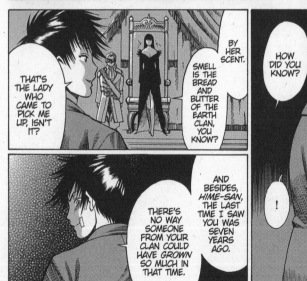

THAT'S THE LADY WHO CAME TO PICK ME UP, ISN'T IT?

BY HER SCENT.

SMELL IS THE BREAD AND BUTTER OF THE EARTH CLAN, YOU KNOW?

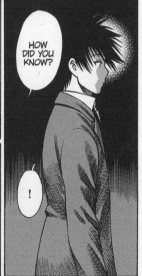

HOW DID YOU KNOW?

!

AND BESIDES, *HIME-SAN*, THE LAST TIME I SAW YOU WAS SEVEN YEARS AGO.

THERE'S NO WAY SOMEONE FROM YOUR CLAN COULD HAVE GROWN SO MUCH IN THAT TIME.

16

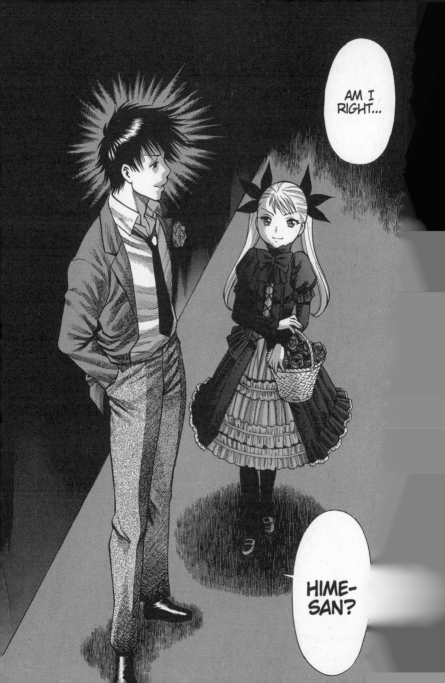

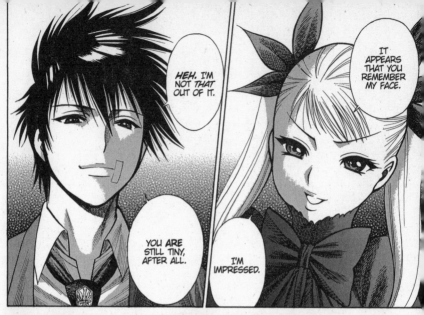

HEH. I'M NOT *THAT* OUT OF IT.

IT APPEARS THAT YOU REMEMBER MY FACE.

YOU ARE STILL TINY, AFTER ALL.

I'M IMPRESSED.

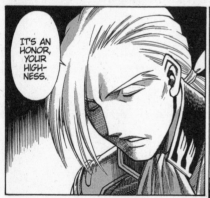

IT'S AN HONOR, YOUR HIGH-NESS.

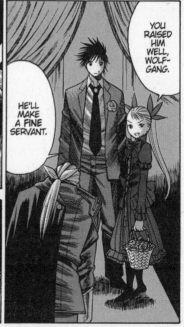

YOU RAISED HIM WELL, WOLF-GANG.

HE'LL MAKE A FINE SERVANT.

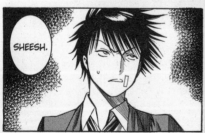

SHEESH.

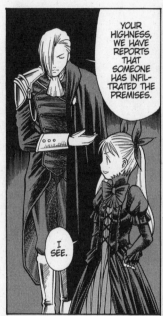

YOUR HIGHNESS, WE HAVE REPORTS THAT SOMEONE HAS INFILTRATED THE PREMISES.

I SEE.

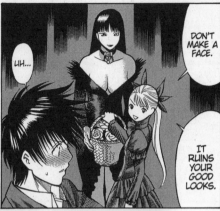

UH...

DON'T MAKE A FACE.

IT RUINS YOUR GOOD LOOKS.

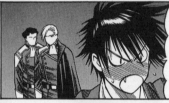

YOU'RE ONE TO TALK!!

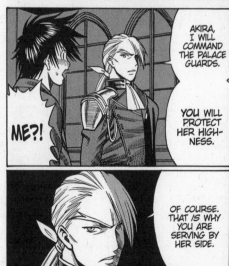

AKIRA, I WILL COMMAND THE PALACE GUARDS.

YOU WILL PROTECT HER HIGHNESS.

ME?!

OF COURSE. THAT IS WHY YOU ARE SERVING BY HER SIDE.

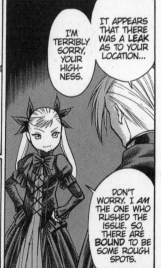

I'M TERRIBLY SORRY, YOUR HIGHNESS.

IT APPEARS THAT THERE WAS A LEAK AS TO YOUR LOCATION...

DON'T WORRY. I AM THE ONE WHO RUSHED THE ISSUE. SO, THERE ARE BOUND TO BE SOME ROUGH SPOTS.

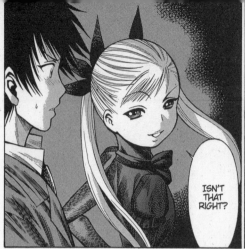

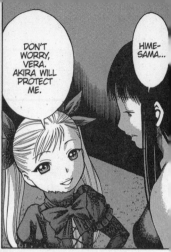

DON'T WORRY, VERA. AKIRA WILL PROTECT ME.

HIME-SAMA...

ISN'T THAT RIGHT?

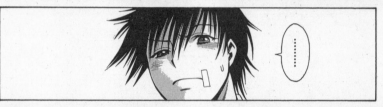

......

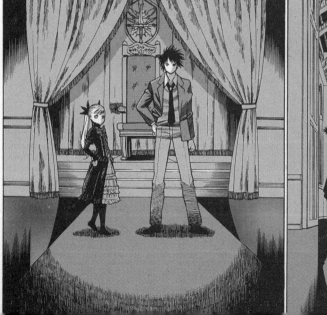

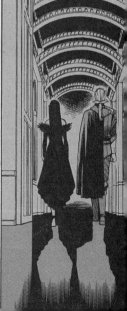

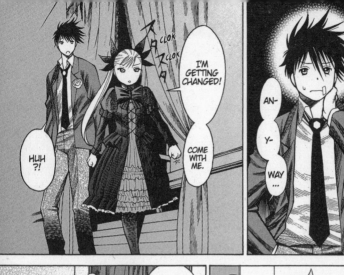

I'M GETTING CHANGED!

COME WITH ME.

HUH ?!

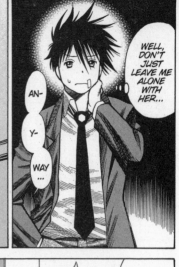

WELL, DON'T JUST LEAVE ME ALONE WITH HER...

AN-Y-WAY...

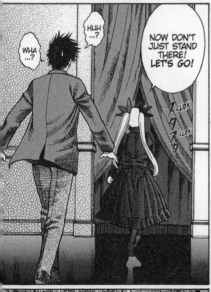

WHA ...?

HUH ...?

NOW DON'T JUST STAND THERE! LET'S GO!

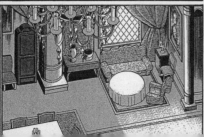

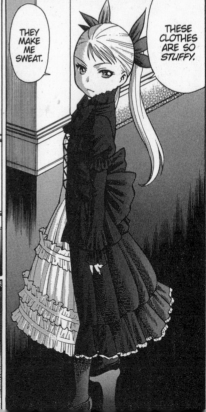

THEY MAKE ME SWEAT.

THESE CLOTHES ARE SO STUFFY.

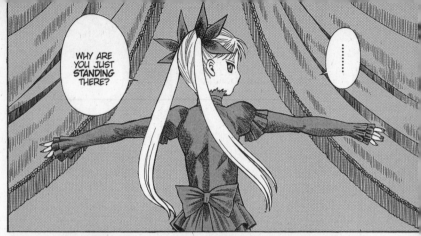

WHY ARE YOU JUST STANDING THERE?

....

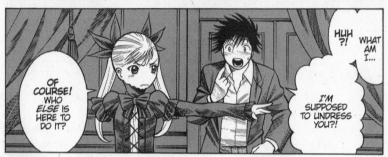

OF COURSE! WHO *ELSE* IS HERE TO DO IT?

HUH ?! WHAT AM I...

I'M SUPPOSED TO UNDRESS YOU?!

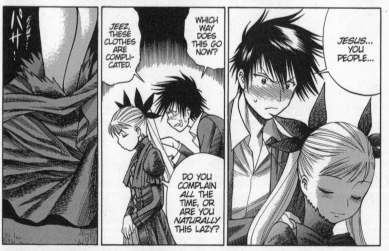

JEEZ, THESE CLOTHES ARE COMPLI-CATED.

WHICH WAY DOES THIS GO NOW?

JESUS... YOU PEOPLE...

DO YOU COMPLAIN ALL THE TIME, OR ARE YOU *NATURALLY* THIS LAZY?

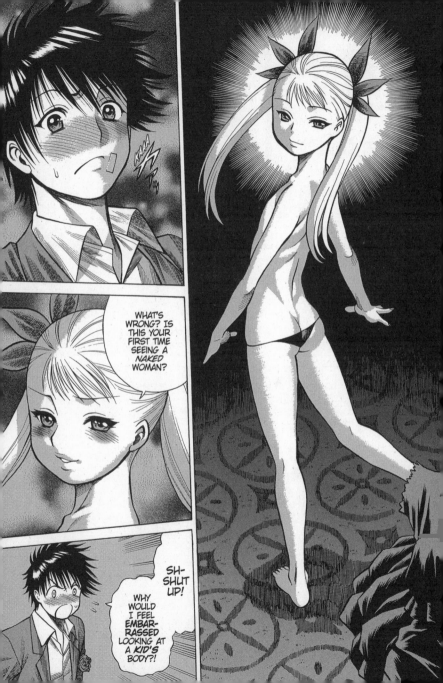

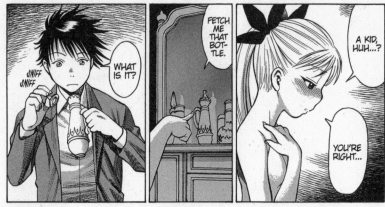

WHAT IS IT?

SNIFF SNIFF

FETCH ME THAT BOTTLE.

A KID, HUH...?

YOU'RE RIGHT...

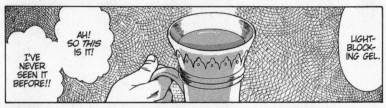

AH! SO *THIS* IS IT!

I'VE NEVER SEEN IT BEFORE!!

LIGHT-BLOCKING GEL.

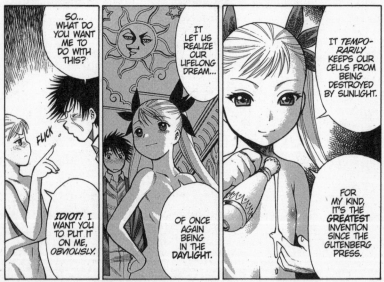

SO... WHAT DO YOU WANT ME TO DO WITH THIS?

FLICK

IDIOT! I WANT YOU TO PUT IT ON ME, OBVIOUSLY.

IT LET US REALIZE OUR LIFELONG DREAM...

OF ONCE AGAIN BEING IN THE DAYLIGHT.

IT *TEMPO-RARILY* KEEPS OUR CELLS FROM BEING DESTROYED BY SUNLIGHT.

FOR MY KIND, IT'S THE **GREATEST** INVENTION SINCE THE GUTENBERG PRESS.

YOU'RE NOT TROUBLED BY A KID'S BODY, ARE YOU?

WHAT'S WRONG?

LIKE I SAID, WHO ELSE IS HERE TO DO IT?!

ME?!

· · · ·

KAAT!V

RELAX... SHE'S JUST A KID... ONLY A KID...

NO, OF COURSE NOT! I'M FINE!

IT'S NO BIG DEAL...

....

WHAT HAPPENED TO YOUR CHEEK?

IT WAS WHERE I GOT PUNCHED.

THIS.

GUESS IT'S GONE NOW.

HMM?

OH...

OF COURSE I *DIDN'T*. IT WAS AN OLD FRIEND OF MINE...

AND I WAS THE BAD GUY.

WHO DID YOU FIGHT? I ASSUME YOU *KILLED* HIM, OF COURSE.

REALLY NOW? I DIDN'T THINK THERE WOULD BE *ANYONE* HERE ABLE TO HURT A MEMBER OF THE EARTH CLAN.

WHAT DID YOU DO?

HE SAID THAT I TOYED WITH YUKI'S...

WELL... A FRIEND'S FEELINGS.

HE ASKED ME IF I REALLY HAD HUMAN BLOOD IN ME.

HEH... THAT RYOHEI, HE'S AWFULLY SHARP, I'LL GIVE HIM THAT.

PLEASE DO...

WAIT.

I'LL DO THE FRONT MYSELF.

THAT GIRL...DID YOU TOY WITH HER?

HUH?

SO, DID YOU TOY WITH HER?

......

......

I DIDN'T LAY A FINGER ON HER!!

HELL NO!

28

I DIDN'T DO ANYTHING. I'M NOT ALLOWED...

TO DO ANYTHING.

YEAH. YOU'RE RIGHT.

FROM THE MOMENT YOU WERE BORN, YOU WERE MEANT TO SERVE ME.

OF COURSE.

THE EARTH CLAN HAS SERVED US FOR GENERATIONS.

BUT TO BE HONEST, THAT'S REALLY NOT IMPORTANT.

AS LONG AS I'M ME... I CAN'T BE CLOSE TO ANYONE.

THE REAL BURDEN IS THE BLOOD THAT RUNS THROUGH MY VEINS.

SUCH A PETTY CONCERN.

GIVE ME YOUR HAND...

MY, AKIRA...

YOU'VE REALLY GROWN.

HIME-...?

SAN?

HUH?

AND SO IT BEGINS.

!

BOTH HUMAN AND NON-HUMAN.

THERE ARE A LOT OF PEOPLE OUT THERE WHO WANT ME DEAD...

SNIFF

WE MUST LEAVE AT ONCE...!

YOUR HIGHNESS, THE INTRUDERS ARE APPROACHING!

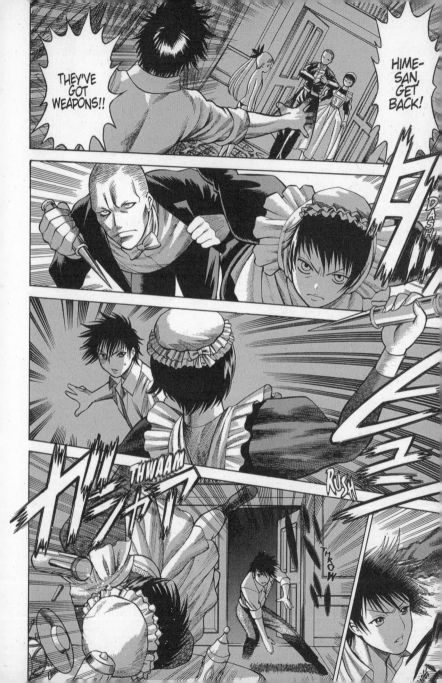

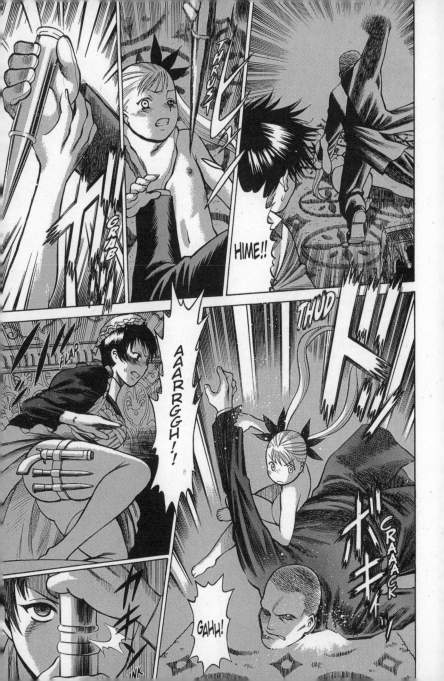

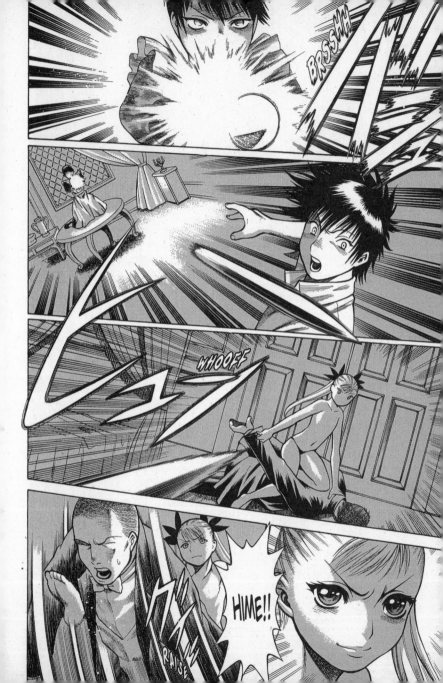

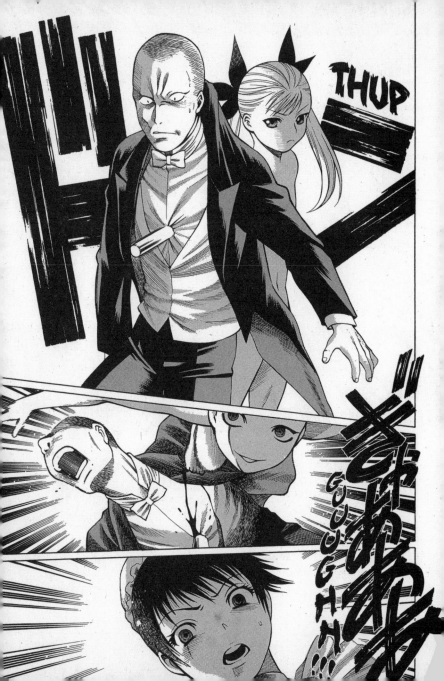

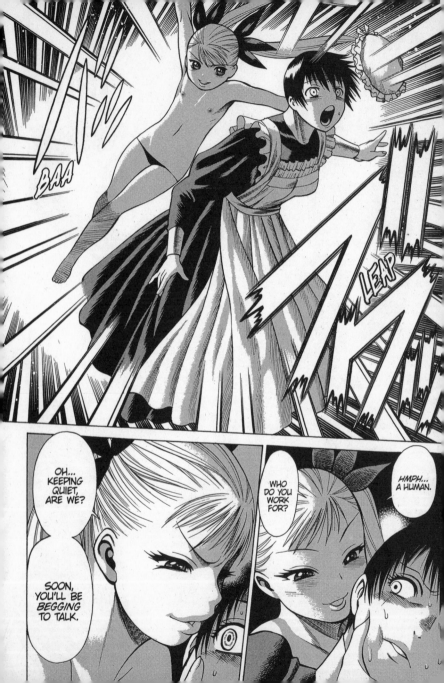

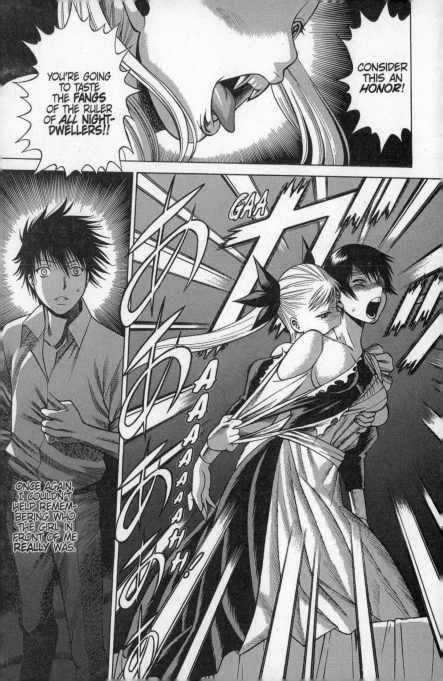

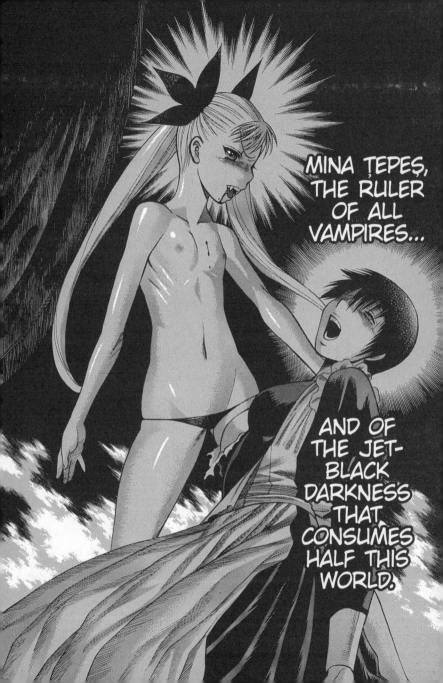

MINA ȚEPEȘ, THE RULER OF ALL VAMPIRES...

AND OF THE JET-BLACK DARKNESS THAT CONSUMES HALF THIS WORLD.

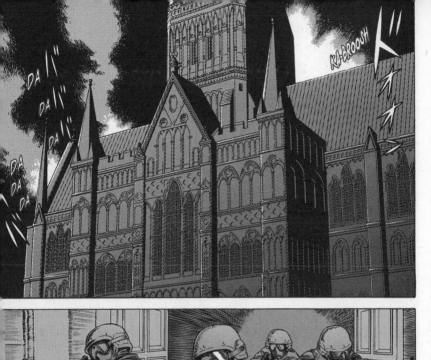

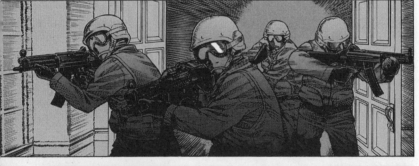

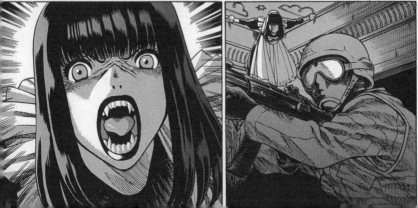

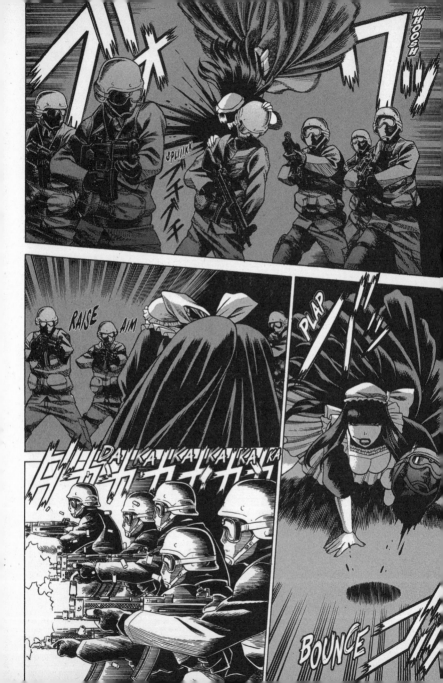

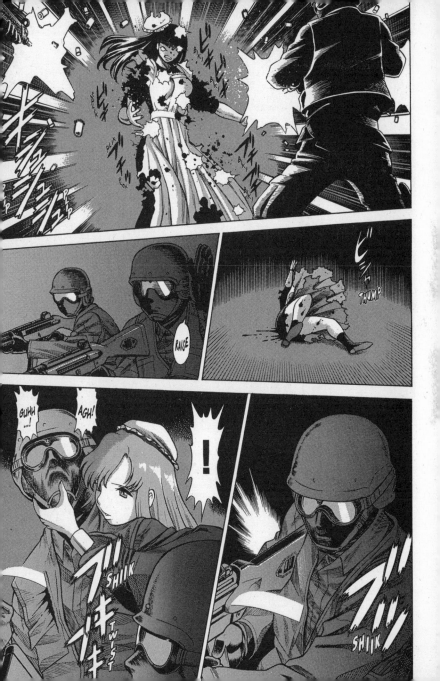

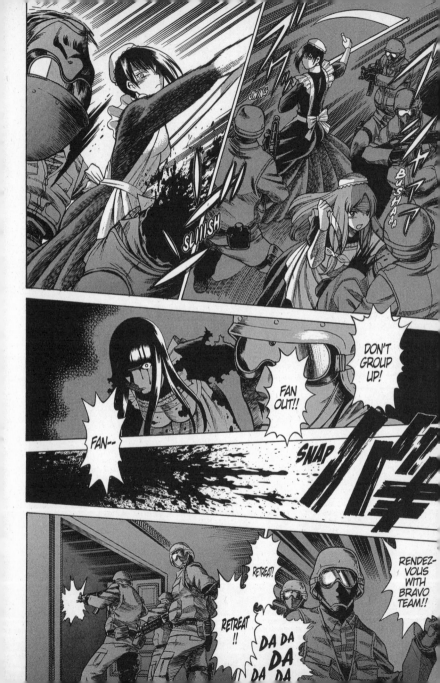

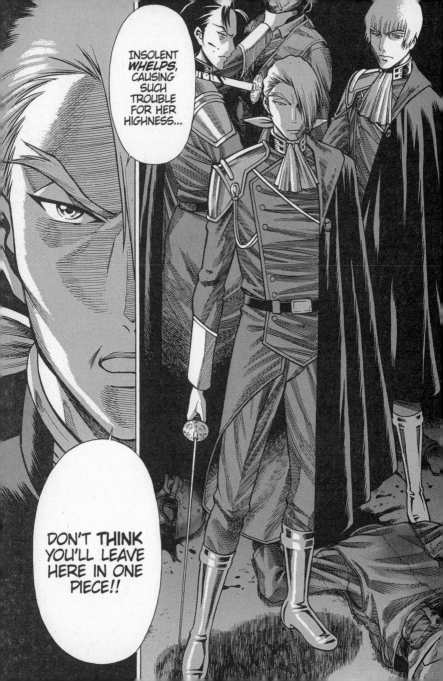

Chapter 2: Choice

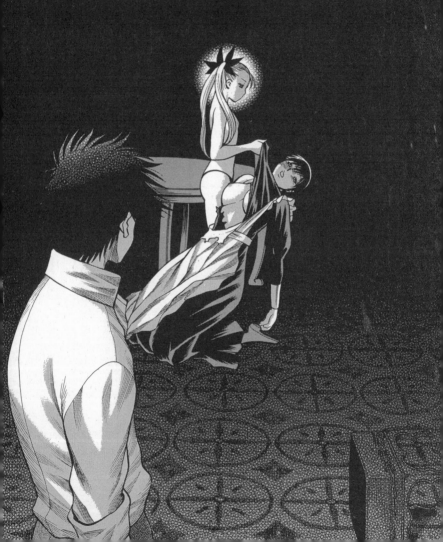

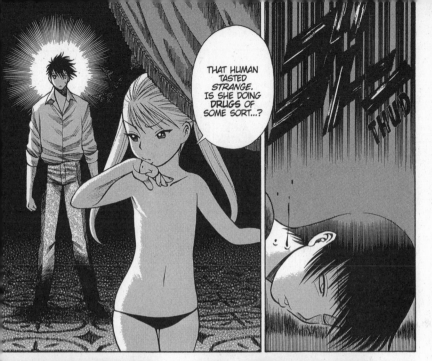

THAT HUMAN TASTED *STRANGE.* IS SHE DOING *DRUGS* OF SOME SORT...?

THUD

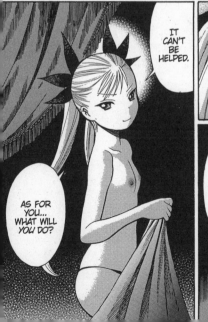

IT CAN'T BE HELPED.

AS FOR YOU... WHAT WILL *YOU* DO?

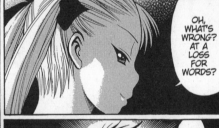

OH, WHAT'S WRONG? AT A LOSS FOR WORDS?

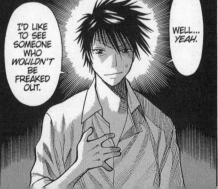

I'D LIKE TO SEE SOMEONE WHO *WOULDN'T* BE FREAKED OUT.

WELL... YEAH.

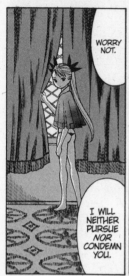

WORRY NOT.

I DON'T WANT TROUBLE LATER.

ARE YOU SERIOUS?

LEAVE.

IF YOU DON'T INTEND TO BE MY SERVANT, THAT'S FINE. YOU CAN STILL GO BACK.

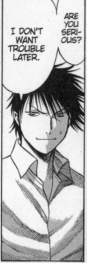

I WILL NEITHER PURSUE NOR CONDEMN YOU.

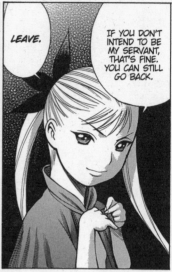

!

GOOD TIMING.

I SHALL GO AND *BASK* IN THE LIGHT OF DAWN.

HMM, IT'S ALMOST DAWN.

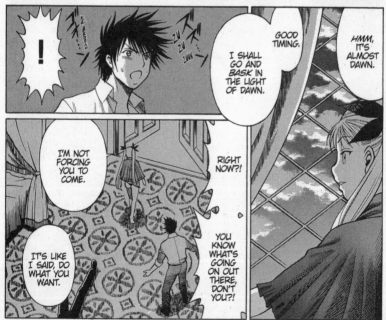

I'M NOT FORCING YOU TO COME.

RIGHT NOW?!

IT'S LIKE I SAID, DO WHAT YOU WANT.

YOU KNOW WHAT'S GOING ON OUT THERE, DON'T YOU?!

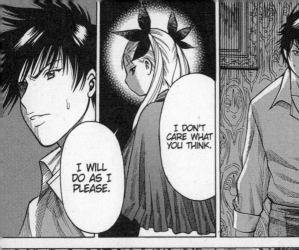

I DON'T CARE WHAT YOU THINK.

I WILL DO AS I PLEASE.

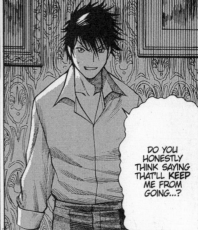

DO YOU HONESTLY THINK SAYING THAT'LL **KEEP** ME FROM GOING...?

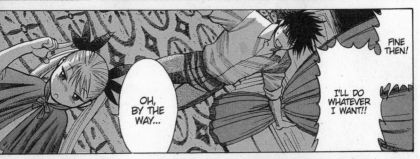

OH, BY THE WAY...

FINE THEN!

I'LL DO WHATEVER I WANT!!

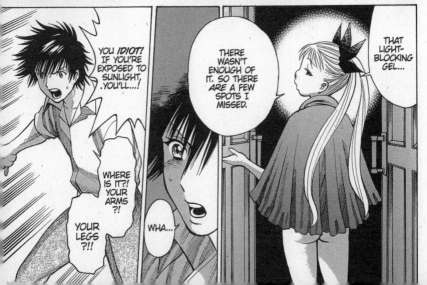

YOU *IDIOT!* IF YOU'RE EXPOSED TO SUNLIGHT, YOU'LL....!

THERE WASN'T ENOUGH OF IT. SO THERE ARE A FEW SPOTS I MISSED.

THAT LIGHT-BLOCKING GEL...

WHERE IS IT?! YOUR ARMS?!

YOUR LEGS?!!

WHA...

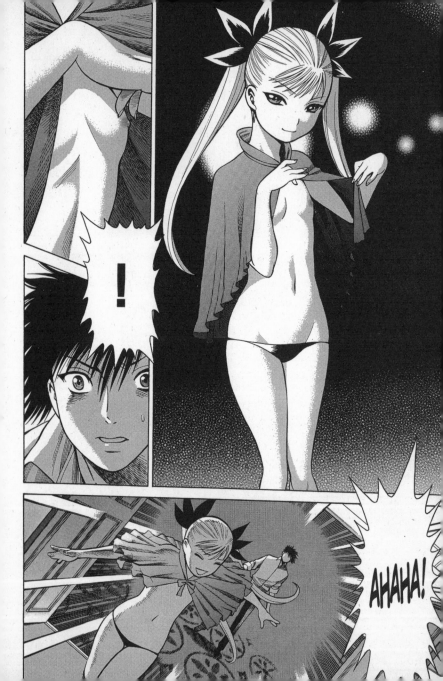

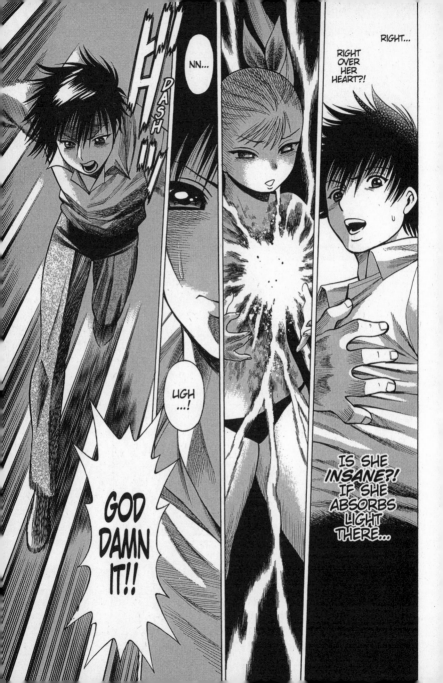

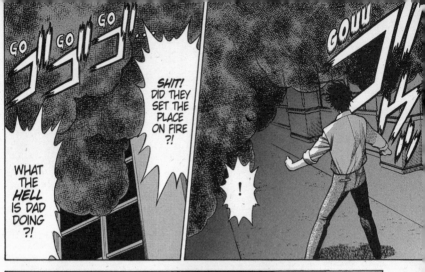

GO GO GO ゴゴゴゴ

GOUU ゴウウ

SHIT! DID THEY SET THE PLACE ON FIRE?!

WHAT THE *HELL* IS DAD DOING?!

!

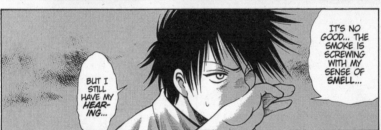

IT'S NO GOOD... THE SMOKE IS SCREWING WITH MY SENSE OF SMELL...

BUT I STILL HAVE MY *HEAR-ING...*

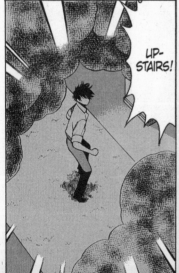

UP-STAIRS!

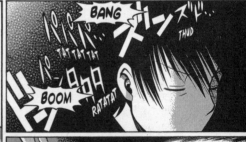

BANG

スパーンズ

THUD

TAT TAT TAT

BOOM

RATATAT

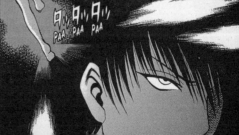

PAA PAA PAA

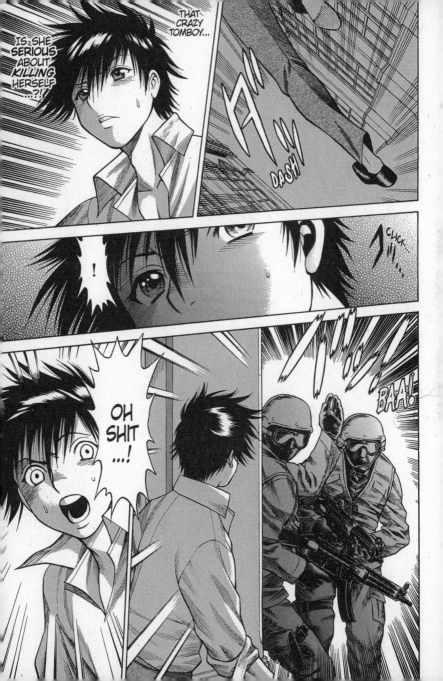

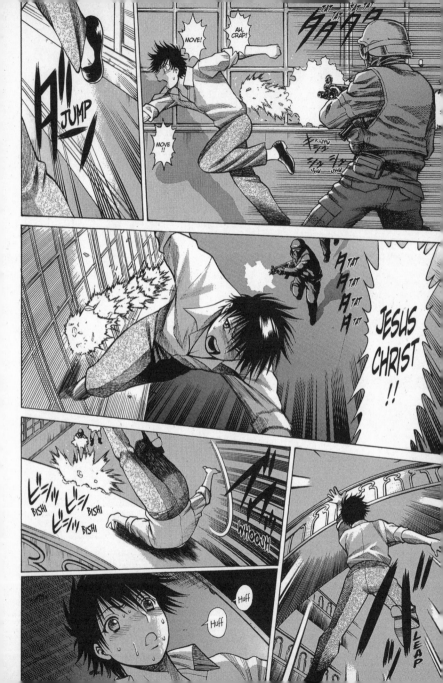

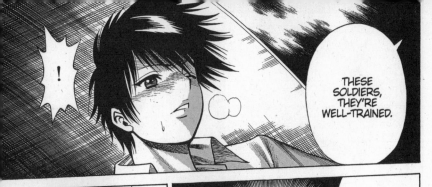

THESE SOLDIERS, THEY'RE WELL-TRAINED.

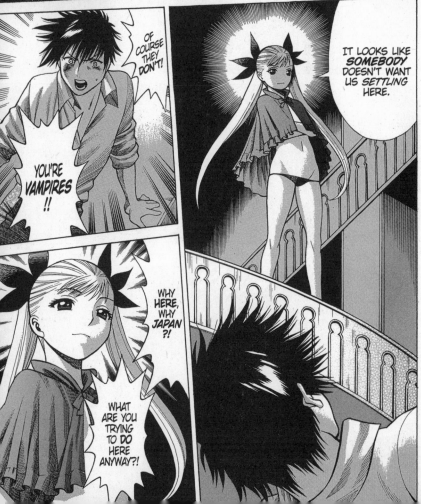

OF COURSE THEY DON'T!

YOU'RE VAMPIRES!!

IT LOOKS LIKE *SOMEBODY* DOESN'T WANT US *SETTLING* HERE.

WHY HERE, WHY *JAPAN*?!

WHAT ARE YOU TRYING TO DO HERE ANYWAY?!

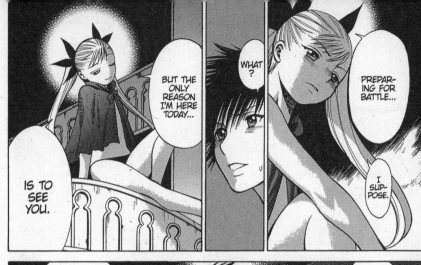

BUT THE ONLY REASON I'M HERE TODAY...

WHAT?

PREPARING FOR BATTLE...

I SUPPOSE.

IS TO SEE YOU.

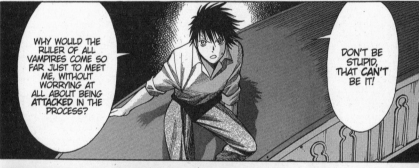

WHY WOULD THE RULER OF ALL VAMPIRES COME SO FAR JUST TO MEET ME, WITHOUT WORRYING AT ALL ABOUT BEING ATTACKED IN THE PROCESS?

DON'T BE STUPID, THAT *CAN'T* BE IT!

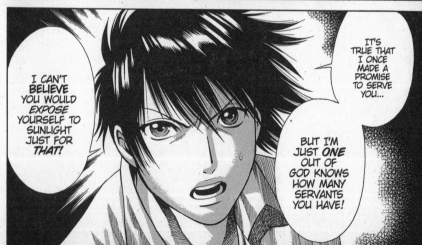

I CAN'T *BELIEVE* YOU WOULD *EXPOSE* YOURSELF TO SUNLIGHT JUST FOR *THAT*!

IT'S TRUE THAT I ONCE MADE A PROMISE TO SERVE YOU...

BUT I'M JUST *ONE* OUT OF GOD KNOWS HOW MANY SERVANTS YOU HAVE!

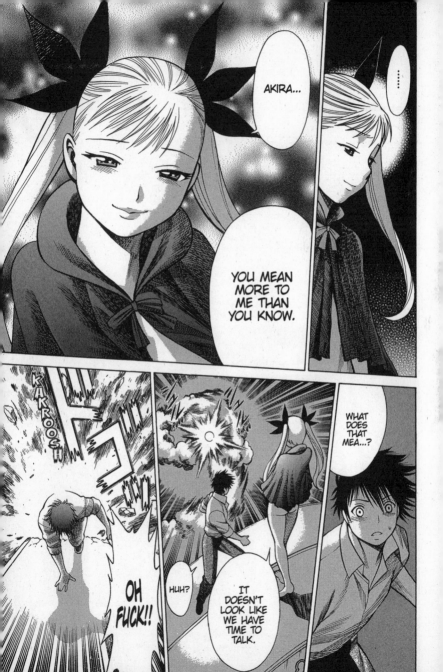

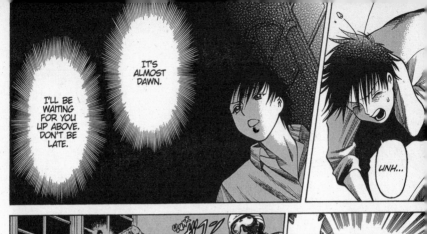

IT'S ALMOST DAWN.

I'LL BE WAITING FOR YOU UP ABOVE. DON'T BE LATE.

UNH...

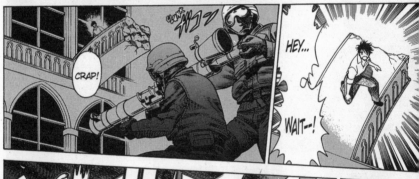

CRAP!

CLINK

HEY...

WAIT--!

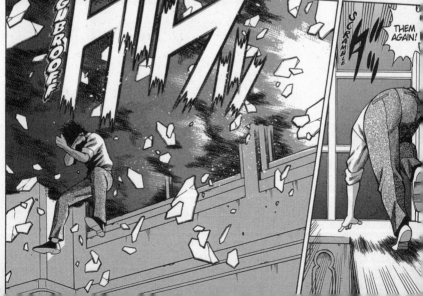

GIBROOFF

DOOM

SCRAMBLE

THEM AGAIN!

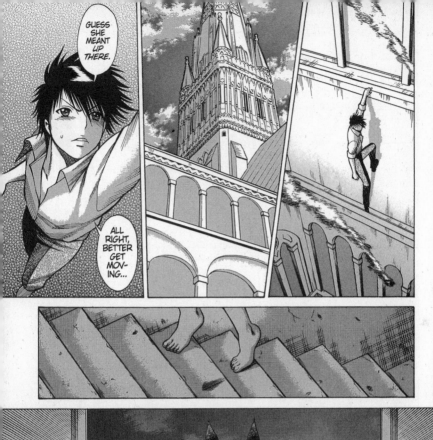

GUESS SHE MEANT UP THERE.

ALL RIGHT, BETTER GET MOV-ING...

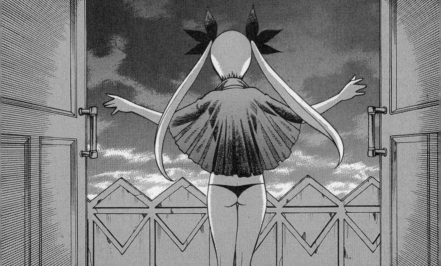

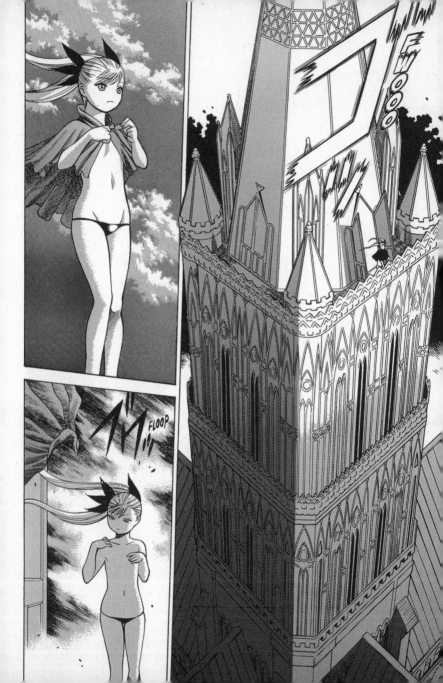

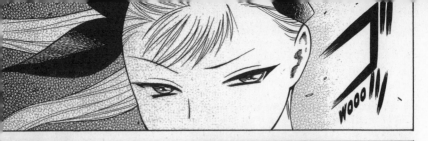

WOOO

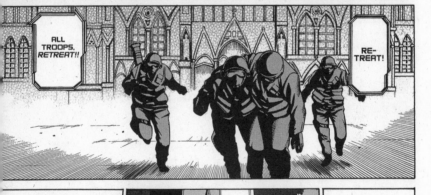

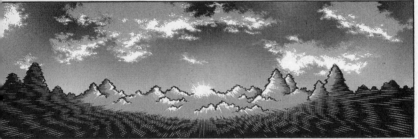

ALL TROOPS, RETREAT!!

RE-TREAT!

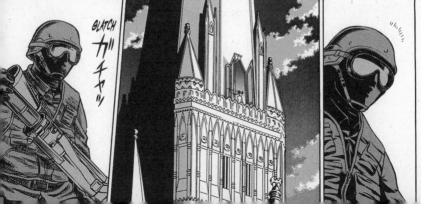

SLATCH

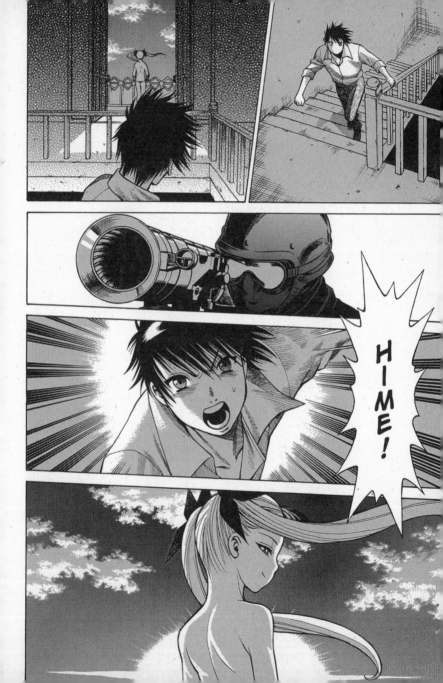

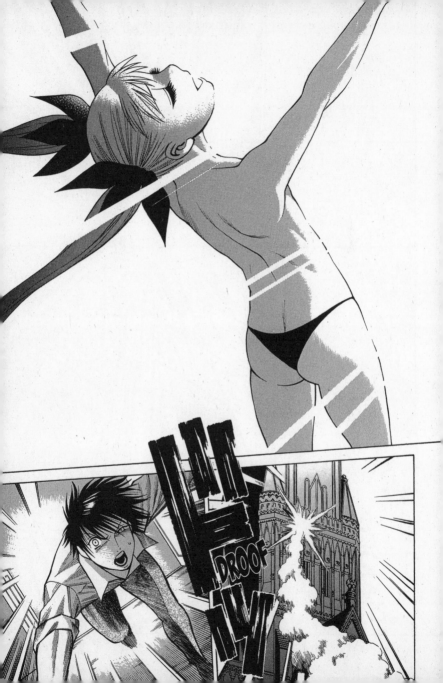

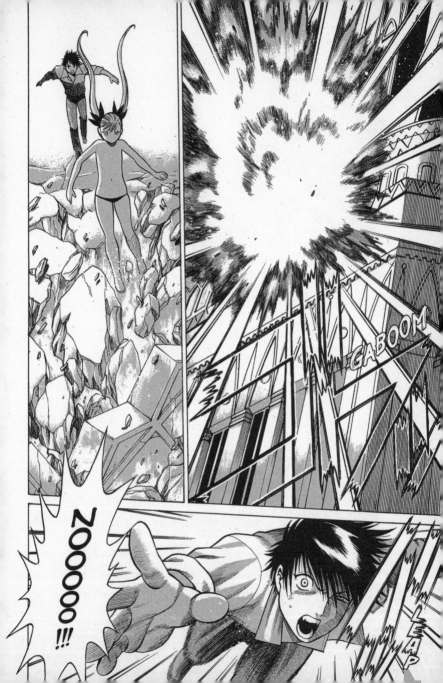

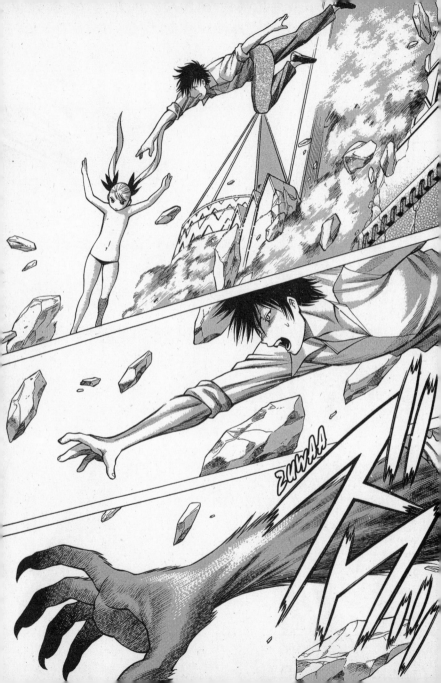

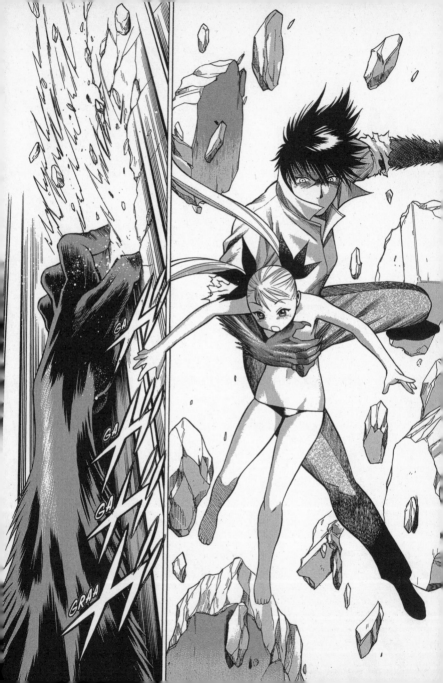

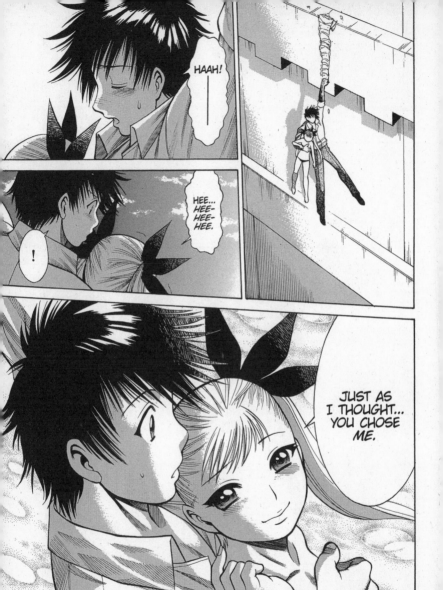

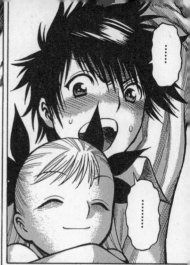

......

......

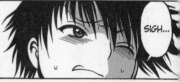

SIGH...

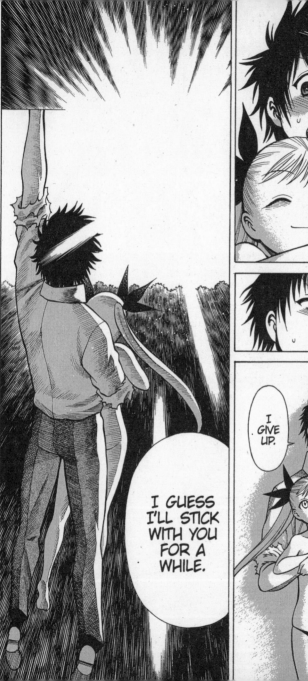

I GUESS I'LL STICK WITH YOU FOR A WHILE.

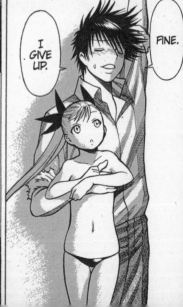

I GIVE UP.

FINE.

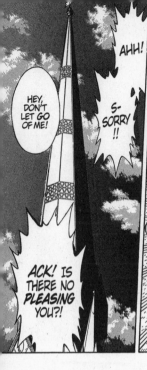

HEY, DON'T LET GO OF ME!

AHH!

S-SORRY!!

ACK! IS THERE NO *PLEASING* YOU?!

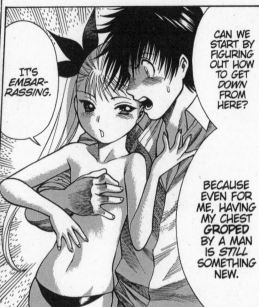

IT'S EMBAR-RASSING.

CAN WE START BY FIGURING OUT HOW TO GET *DOWN* FROM HERE?

BECAUSE EVEN FOR ME, HAVING MY CHEST GROPED BY A MAN IS *STILL* SOMETHING NEW.

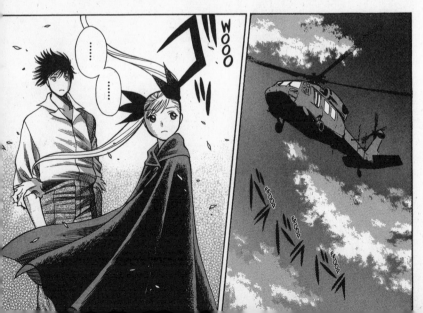

......

......

WOOO

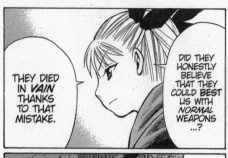

THEY DIED IN *VAIN* THANKS TO THAT MISTAKE.

DID THEY HONESTLY BELIEVE THAT THEY COULD BEST US WITH *NORMAL* WEAPONS ...?

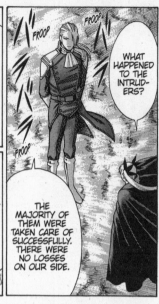

WHAT HAPPENED TO THE INTRUDERS?

FROOP FROOP

FROOP

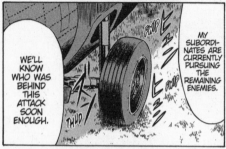

WE'LL KNOW WHO WAS BEHIND THIS ATTACK SOON ENOUGH.

MY SUBORDINATES ARE CURRENTLY PURSUING THE REMAINING ENEMIES.

FRUP

THUD

FRUP

THE MAJORITY OF THEM WERE TAKEN CARE OF SUCCESSFULLY. THERE WERE NO LOSSES ON OUR SIDE.

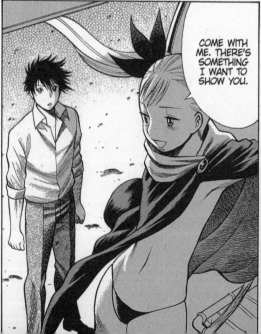

COME WITH ME. THERE'S SOMETHING I WANT TO SHOW YOU.

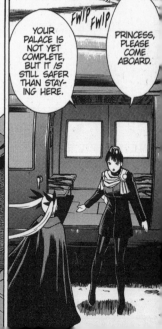

YOUR PALACE IS NOT YET COMPLETE, BUT IT *IS* STILL SAFER THAN STAYING HERE.

PRINCESS, PLEASE COME ABOARD.

FWIP FWIP

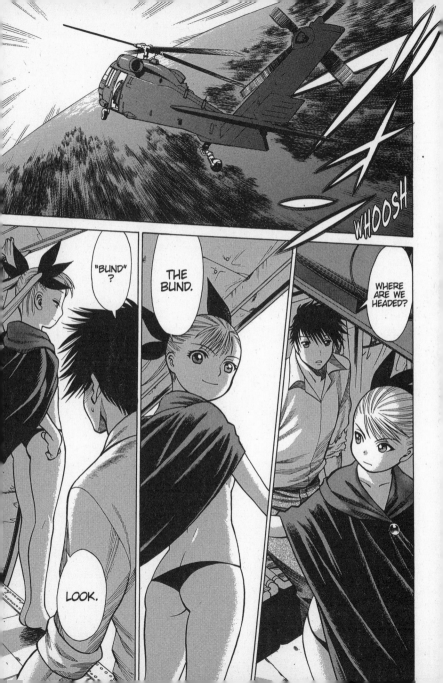

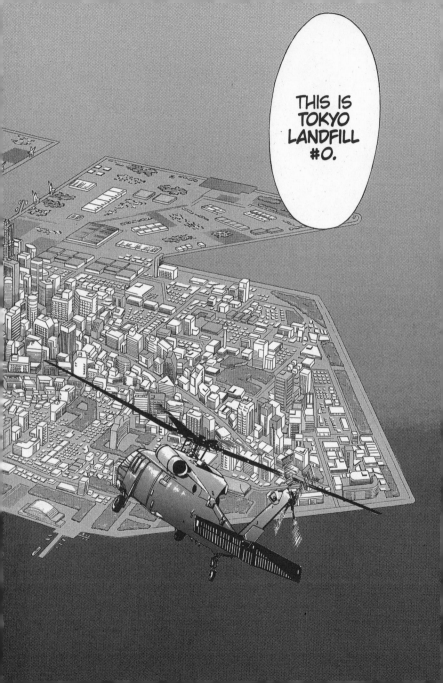

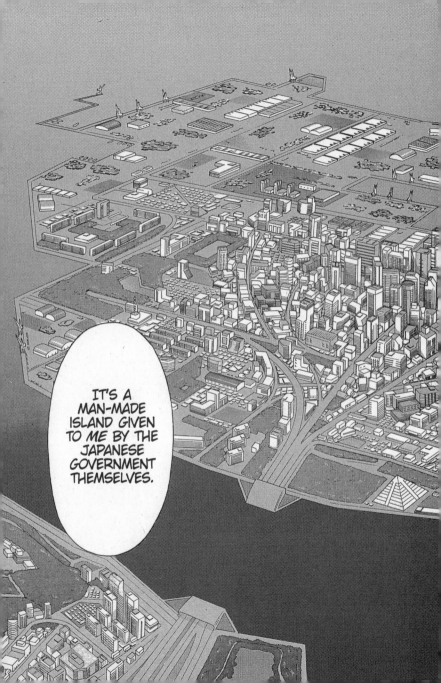

IT'S A MAN-MADE ISLAND GIVEN TO *ME* BY THE JAPANESE GOVERNMENT THEMSELVES.

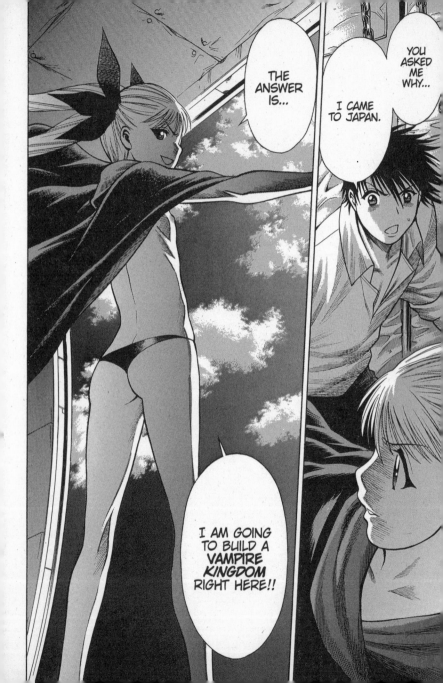

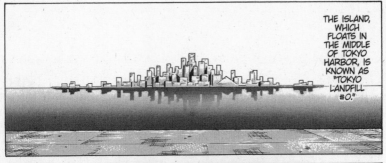

THE ISLAND, WHICH FLOATS IN THE MIDDLE OF TOKYO HARBOR, IS KNOWN AS "TOKYO LANDFILL #0."

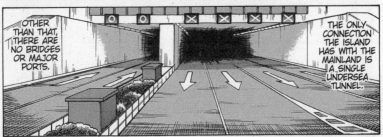

OTHER THAN THAT, THERE ARE NO BRIDGES OR MAJOR PORTS.

THE ONLY CONNECTION THE ISLAND HAS WITH THE MAINLAND IS A SINGLE UNDERSEA TUNNEL.

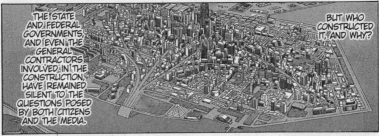

THE STATE AND FEDERAL GOVERNMENTS, AND EVEN THE GENERAL CONTRACTORS INVOLVED IN THE CONSTRUCTION, HAVE REMAINED SILENT TO THE QUESTIONS POSED BY BOTH CITIZENS AND THE MEDIA.

BUT WHO CONSTRUCTED IT, AND WHY?

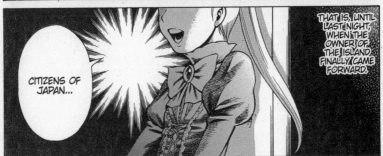

THAT IS, UNTIL LAST NIGHT, WHEN THE OWNER OF THE ISLAND FINALLY CAME FORWARD.

CITIZENS OF JAPAN...

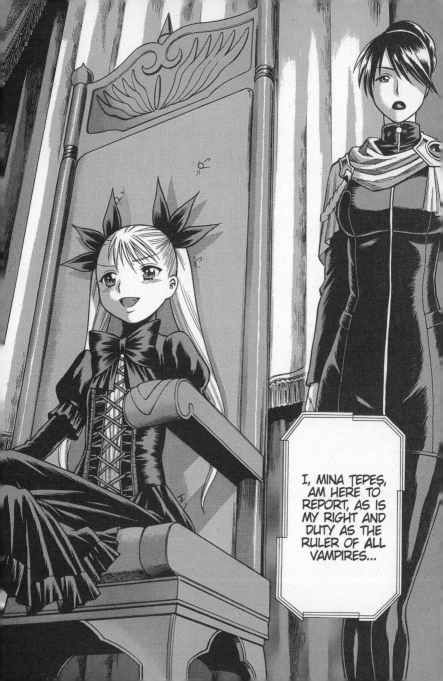

I, MINA TEPES, AM HERE TO REPORT, AS IS MY RIGHT AND DUTY AS THE RULER OF ALL VAMPIRES...

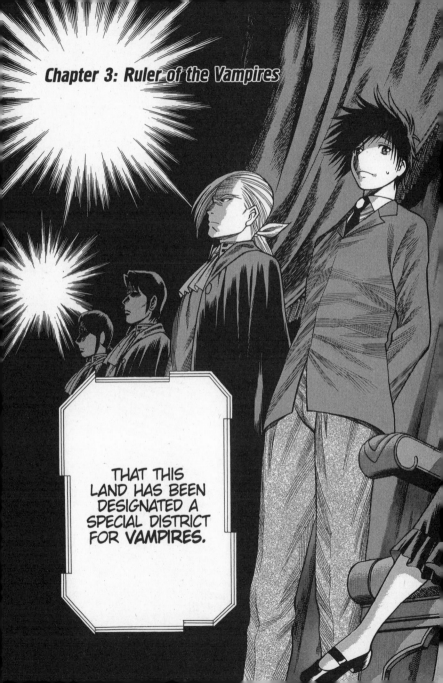

Chapter 3: Ruler of the Vampires

THAT THIS LAND HAS BEEN DESIGNATED A SPECIAL DISTRICT FOR VAMPIRES.

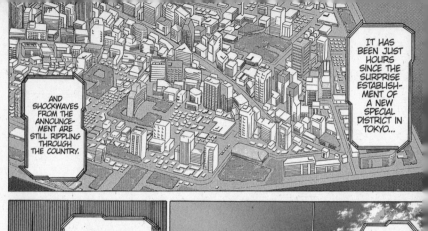

IT HAS BEEN JUST HOURS SINCE THE SURPRISE ESTABLISHMENT OF A NEW SPECIAL DISTRICT IN TOKYO...

AND SHOCKWAVES FROM THE ANNOUNCEMENT ARE STILL RIPPLING THROUGH THE COUNTRY.

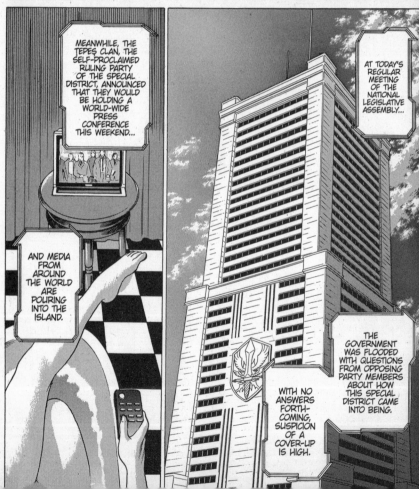

MEANWHILE, THE TEPES CLAN, THE SELF-PROCLAIMED RULING PARTY OF THE SPECIAL DISTRICT, ANNOUNCED THAT THEY WOULD BE HOLDING A WORLD-WIDE PRESS CONFERENCE THIS WEEKEND...

AND MEDIA FROM AROUND THE WORLD ARE POURING INTO THE ISLAND.

AT TODAY'S REGULAR MEETING OF THE NATIONAL LEGISLATIVE ASSEMBLY...

THE GOVERNMENT WAS FLOODED WITH QUESTIONS FROM OPPOSING PARTY MEMBERS ABOUT HOW THIS SPECIAL DISTRICT CAME INTO BEING.

WITH NO ANSWERS FORTHCOMING, SUSPICION OF A COVER-UP IS HIGH.

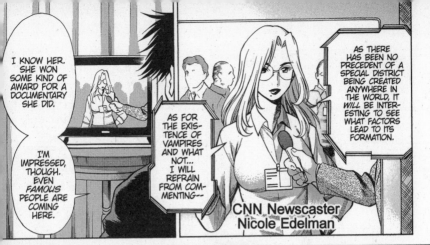

I KNOW HER. SHE WON SOME KIND OF AWARD FOR A DOCUMENTARY SHE DID.

I'M IMPRESSED, THOUGH. EVEN *FAMOUS* PEOPLE ARE COMING HERE.

AS FOR THE EXISTENCE OF VAMPIRES AND WHAT NOT... I WILL REFRAIN FROM COMMENTING--

AS THERE HAS BEEN NO PRECEDENT OF A SPECIAL DISTRICT BEING CREATED ANYWHERE IN THE WORLD, IT *WILL* BE INTERESTING TO SEE WHAT FACTORS LEAD TO ITS FORMATION.

CNN Newscaster
Nicole Edelman

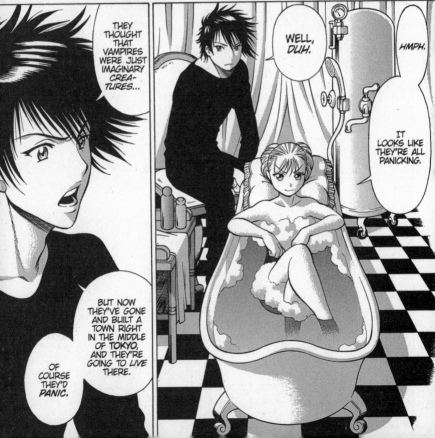

THEY THOUGHT THAT VAMPIRES WERE JUST IMAGINARY CREATURES...

WELL, *DUH.*

HMPH.

IT LOOKS LIKE THEY'RE ALL PANICKING.

BUT NOW THEY'VE GONE AND BUILT A TOWN RIGHT IN THE MIDDLE OF TOKYO, AND THEY'RE GOING TO *LIVE* THERE.

OF COURSE THEY'D *PANIC.*

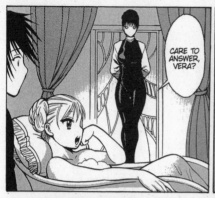

CARE TO ANSWER, VERA?

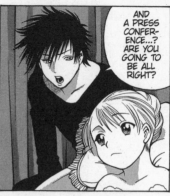

AND A PRESS CONFERENCE...? ARE YOU GOING TO BE ALL RIGHT?

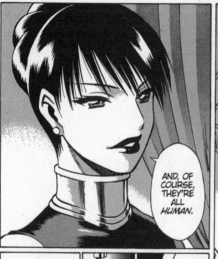

AND, OF COURSE, THEY'RE ALL *HUMAN*.

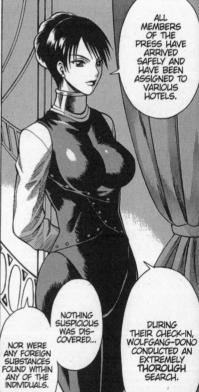

ALL MEMBERS OF THE PRESS HAVE ARRIVED SAFELY AND HAVE BEEN ASSIGNED TO VARIOUS HOTELS.

DURING THEIR CHECK-IN, WOLFGANG-DONO CONDUCTED AN EXTREMELY *THOROUGH* SEARCH.

NOTHING SUSPICIOUS WAS DIS-COVERED...

NOR WERE ANY FOREIGN SUBSTANCES FOUND WITHIN ANY OF THE INDIVIDUALS.

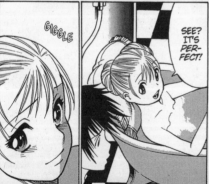

GIGGLE

SEE? IT'S PERFECT!

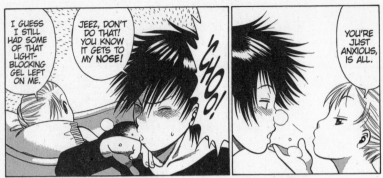

I GUESS I STILL HAD SOME OF THAT LIGHT-BLOCKING GEL LEFT ON ME.

JEEZ, DON'T DO THAT! YOU KNOW IT GETS TO MY NOSE!

'CHOO!

YOU'RE JUST ANXIOUS, IS ALL.

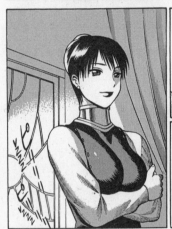

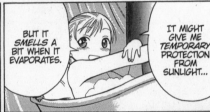

BUT IT SMELLS A BIT WHEN IT EVAPORATES.

IT MIGHT GIVE ME TEMPORARY PROTECTION FROM SUNLIGHT...

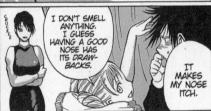

I DON'T SMELL ANYTHING. I GUESS HAVING A GOOD NOSE HAS ITS DRAW-BACKS.

IT MAKES MY NOSE ITCH.

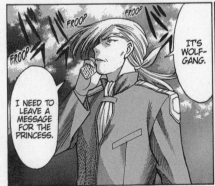

FROOP FROOP FROOP FROOP

IT'S WOLF-GANG.

I NEED TO LEAVE A MESSAGE FOR THE PRINCESS.

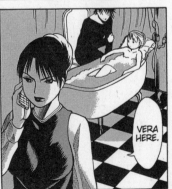

VERA HERE.

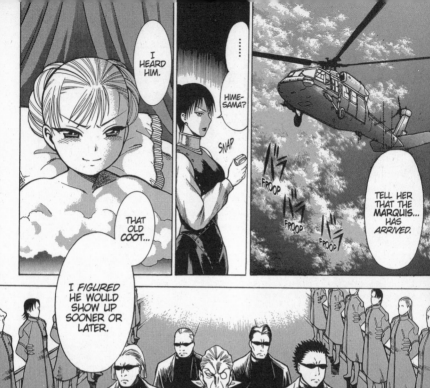

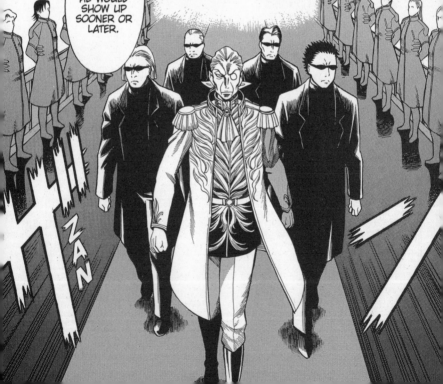

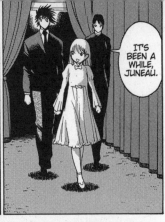

I, JUNEAU, LORD OF DERMAILLE, AM HONORED TO HAVE THE PRIVILEGE OF SEEING YOUR FACE YET AGAIN.

YOUR HIGHNESS...

IT'S BEEN A WHILE, JUNEAU.

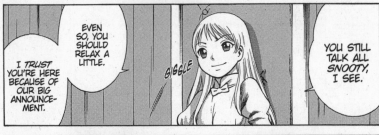

EVEN SO, YOU SHOULD RELAX A LITTLE.

I *TRUST* YOU'RE HERE BECAUSE OF OUR BIG ANNOUNCEMENT.

GIGGLE

YOU STILL TALK ALL *SNOOTY*, I SEE.

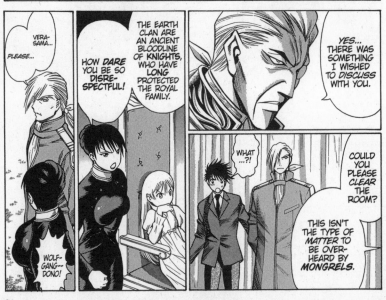

VERA-SAMA...

PLEASE...

HOW *DARE* YOU BE SO DISRESPECTFUL!

THE EARTH CLAN ARE AN ANCIENT BLOODLINE OF KNIGHTS, WHO HAVE LONG PROTECTED THE ROYAL FAMILY.

YES... THERE WAS SOMETHING I WISHED TO *DISCUSS* WITH YOU.

WHAT ...?!

COULD YOU PLEASE *CLEAR* THE ROOM?

THIS ISN'T THE TYPE OF *MATTER* TO BE OVERHEARD BY *MONGRELS*.

WOLF-GANG---DONO!

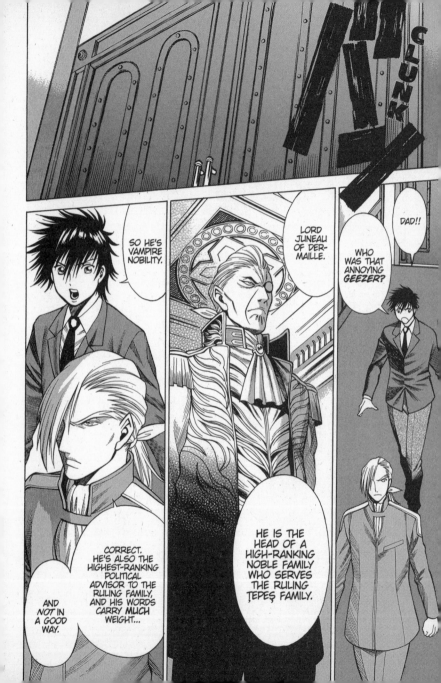

CLUNK

SO HE'S VAMPIRE NOBILITY.

LORD JUNEAU OF DER-MAILLE.

WHO WAS THAT ANNOYING GEEZER?

DAD!!

CORRECT. HE'S ALSO THE HIGHEST-RANKING POLITICAL ADVISOR TO THE RULING FAMILY, AND HIS WORDS CARRY MUCH WEIGHT...

AND NOT IN A GOOD WAY.

HE IS THE HEAD OF A HIGH-RANKING NOBLE FAMILY WHO SERVES THE RULING TEPES FAMILY.

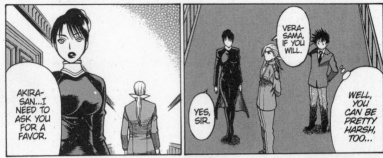

AKIRA-SAN...I NEED TO ASK YOU FOR A FAVOR.

VERA-SAMA, IF YOU WILL.

YES, SIR.

WELL, YOU CAN BE PRETTY HARSH, TOO...

......

ME?

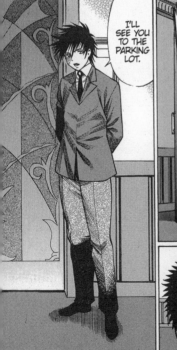

I'LL SEE YOU TO THE PARKING LOT.

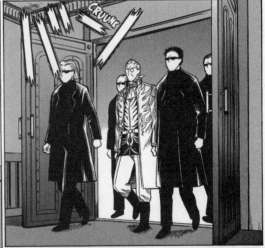

CRUNK

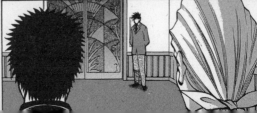

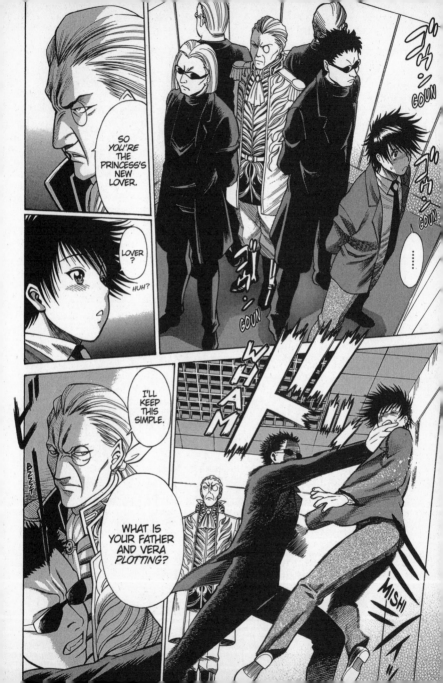

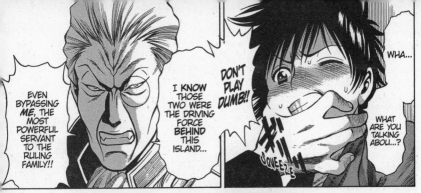

EVEN BYPASSING *ME*, THE MOST POWERFUL SERVANT TO THE RULING FAMILY!!

I KNOW THOSE TWO WERE THE DRIVING FORCE BEHIND THIS ISLAND...

DON'T PLAY *DUMB*!!

SQUEEZE

WHA...

WHAT ARE YOU TALKING ABOU...?

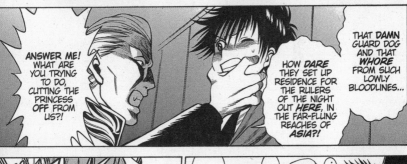

ANSWER ME! WHAT ARE YOU TRYING TO DO, CUTTING THE PRINCESS OFF FROM US?!

HOW *DARE* THEY SET UP RESIDENCE FOR THE RULERS OF THE NIGHT OUT *HERE*, IN THE FAR-FLUNG REACHES OF *ASIA*?!

THAT *DAMN* GUARD DOG AND THAT *WHORE* FROM SUCH LOWLY BLOODLINES...

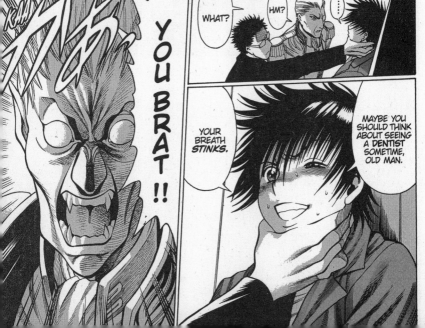

YOU BRAT!!

WHAT?

HM?

......

YOUR BREATH *STINKS*.

MAYBE YOU SHOULD THINK ABOUT SEEING A DENTIST SOMETIME, OLD MAN.

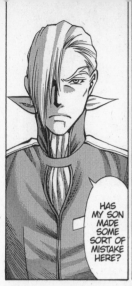
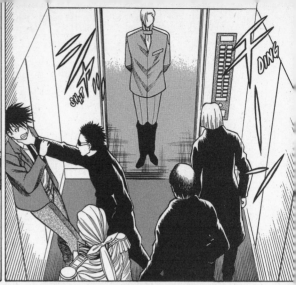

HAS MY SON MADE SOME SORT OF MISTAKE HERE?

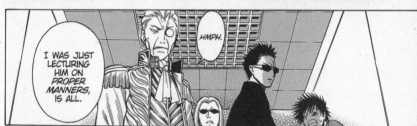

HMPH.

I WAS JUST LECTURING HIM ON *PROPER MANNERS*, IS ALL.

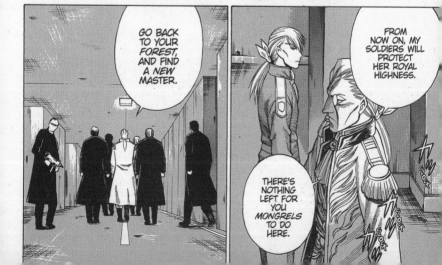

GO BACK TO YOUR *FOREST*, AND FIND A *NEW MASTER*.

FROM NOW ON, MY SOLDIERS WILL PROTECT HER ROYAL HIGHNESS.

THERE'S NOTHING LEFT FOR YOU MONGRELS TO DO HERE.

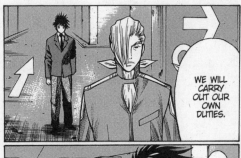

WE WILL CARRY OUT OUR OWN DUTIES.

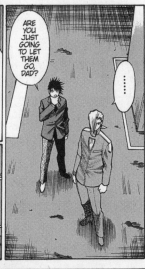

ARE YOU JUST GOING TO LET THEM GO, DAD?

....

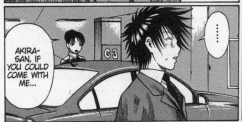

AKIRA-SAN, IF YOU COULD COME WITH ME...

....

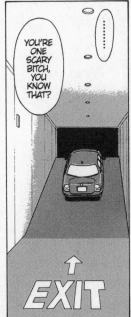

....

YOU'RE ONE SCARY BITCH, YOU KNOW THAT?

EXIT

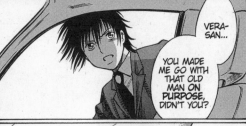

VERA-SAN...

YOU MADE ME GO WITH THAT OLD MAN ON PURPOSE, DIDN'T YOU?

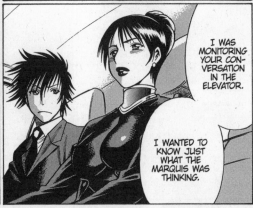

I WAS MONITORING YOUR CONVERSATION IN THE ELEVATOR.

I WANTED TO KNOW JUST WHAT THE MARQUIS WAS THINKING.

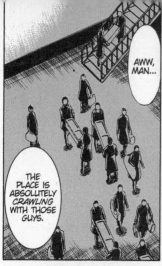

AWW, MAN...

THE PLACE IS ABSOLUTELY CRAWLING WITH THOSE GUYS.

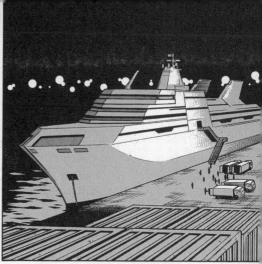

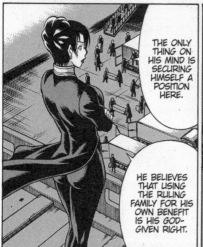

THE ONLY THING ON HIS MIND IS SECURING HIMSELF A POSITION HERE.

HE BELIEVES THAT USING THE RULING FAMILY FOR HIS OWN BENEFIT IS HIS GOD-GIVEN RIGHT.

IS HE TRYING TO FILL THE ENTIRE ISLAND WITH HIS HENCHMEN?

HOW MANY PEOPLE DID HE BRING WITH HIM? HUNDREDS?

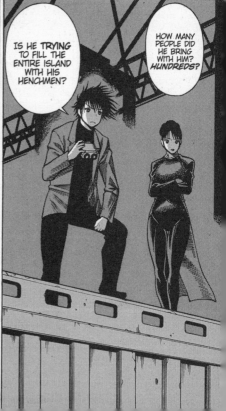

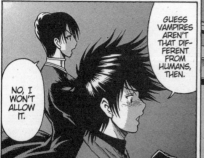

NO, I WON'T ALLOW IT.

GUESS VAMPIRES AREN'T THAT DIF-FERENT FROM HUMANS, THEN.

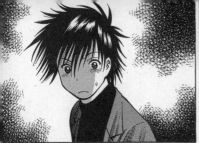

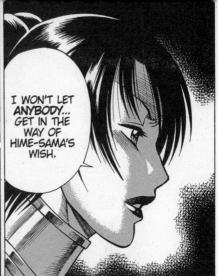

I WON'T LET ANYBODY... GET IN THE WAY OF HIME-SAMA'S WISH.

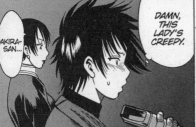

AKIRA-SAN...

DAMN, THIS LADY'S CREEPY.

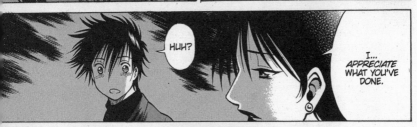

HUH?

I... APPRECIATE WHAT YOU'VE DONE.

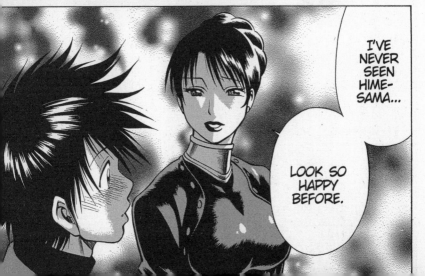

I'VE NEVER SEEN HIME-SAMA...

LOOK SO HAPPY BEFORE.

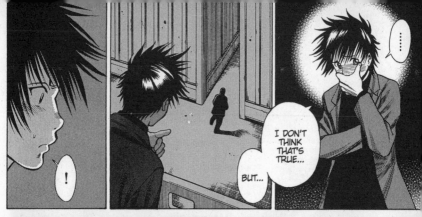

!

I DON'T THINK THAT'S TRUE...

BUT...

......

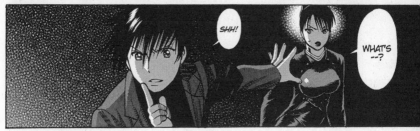

SHH!

WHAT'S --?

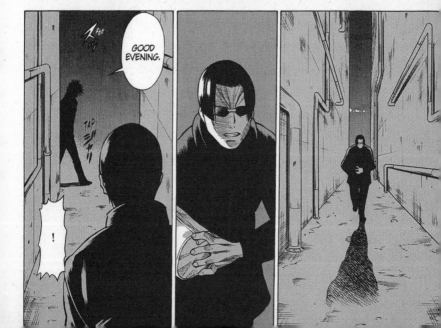

GOOD EVENING.

TAP

!

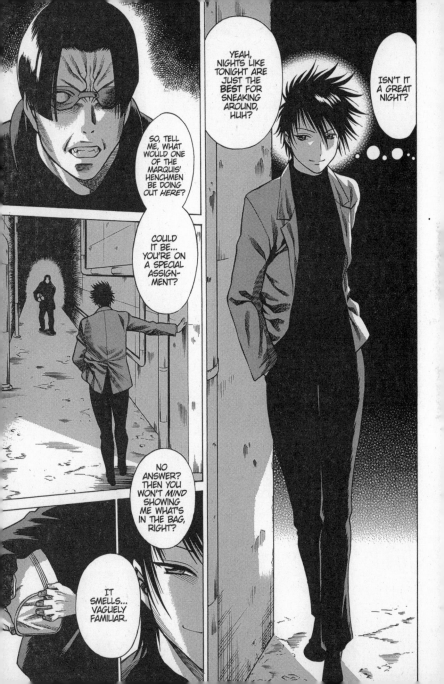

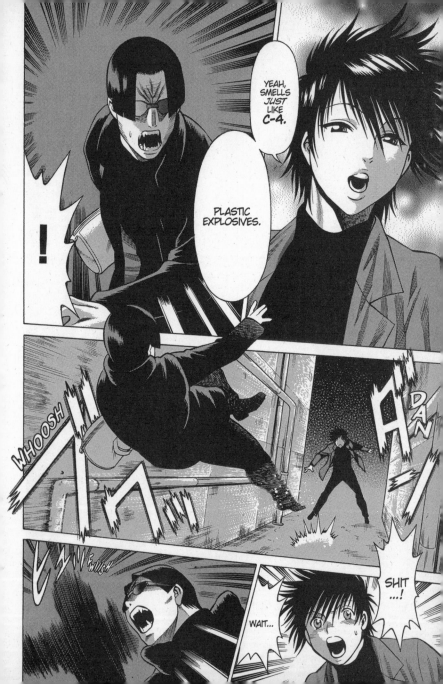

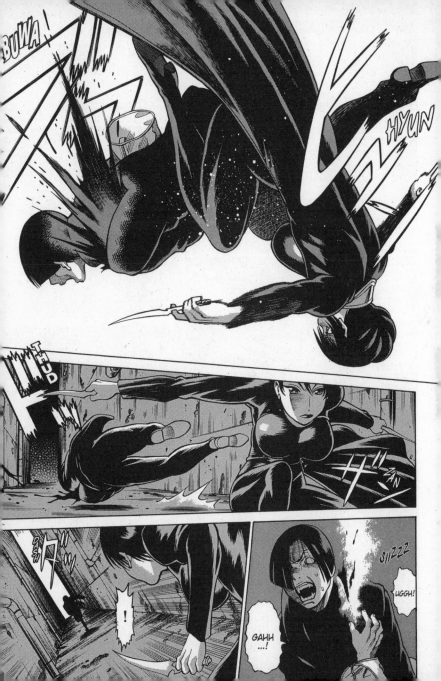

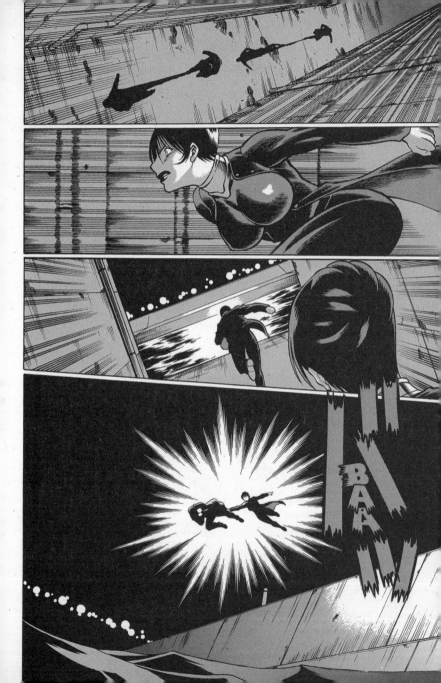

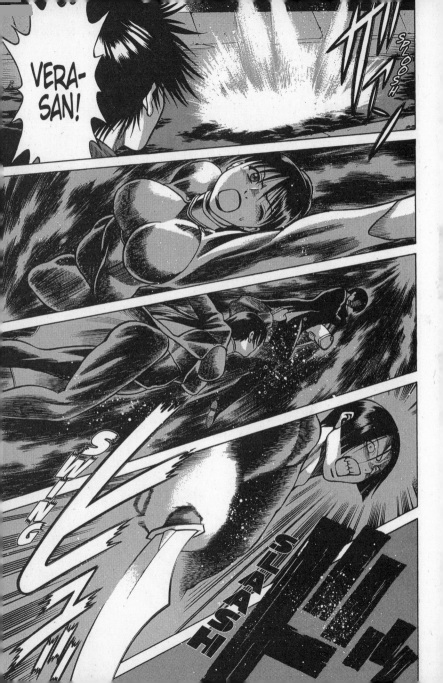

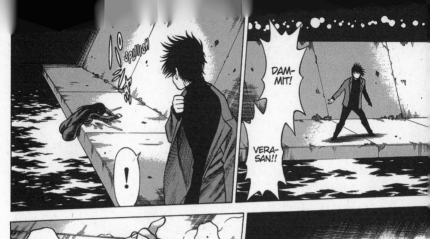

DAM-
MIT!

VERA-
SAN!!

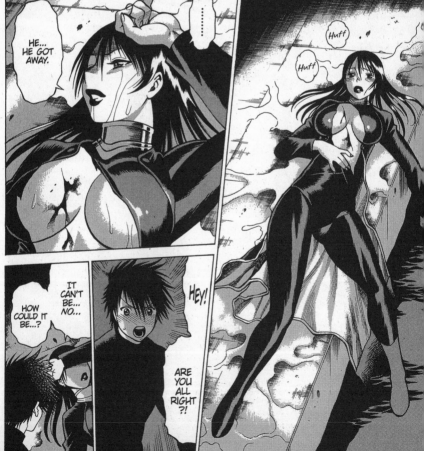

HE...
HE GOT
AWAY.

....

Huff

Huff

IT
CAN'T
BE...
NO...

HOW
COULD IT
BE...?

HEY!

ARE
YOU
ALL
RIGHT
?!

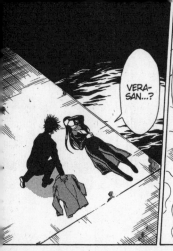

VERA-SAN...?

IT'S IMPOS-SIBLE...

HOW COULD A VAMPIRE BE AFTER HIME-SAMA'S LIFE...?

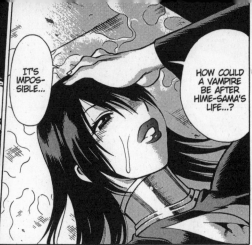

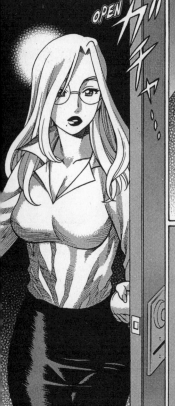

OPEN

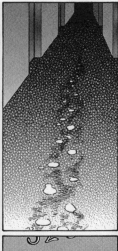

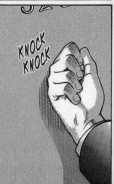

KNOCK KNOCK

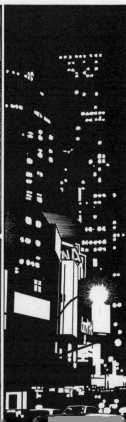

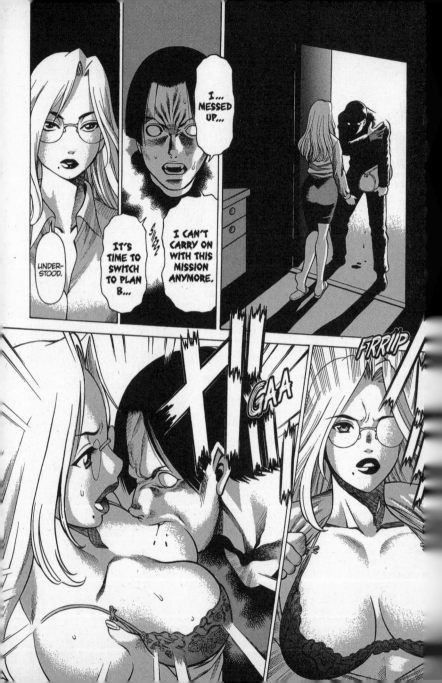

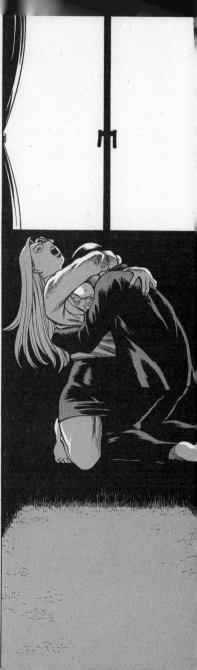

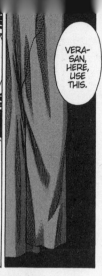

OH... THANK YOU.

VERA-SAN, HERE, USE THIS.

DAD'S SOLDIERS ARE SCOURING THE AREA DOWN BY THE RIVER, BUT THEY HAVEN'T TURNED UP ANYTHING YET.

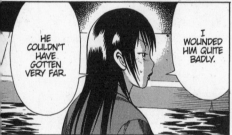

HE COULDN'T HAVE GOTTEN VERY FAR.

I WOUNDED HIM QUITE BADLY.

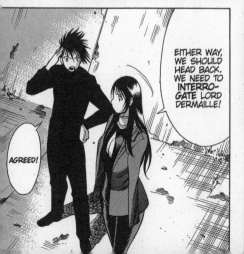

EITHER WAY, WE SHOULD HEAD BACK. WE NEED TO INTERROGATE LORD DERMAILLE!

AGREED!

※ Special Air Service – The British Army's principle special forces unit.

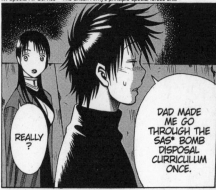

REALLY?

DAD MADE ME GO THROUGH THE SAS* BOMB DISPOSAL CURRICULUM ONCE.

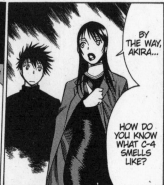

BY THE WAY, AKIRA...

HOW DO YOU KNOW WHAT C-4 SMELLS LIKE?

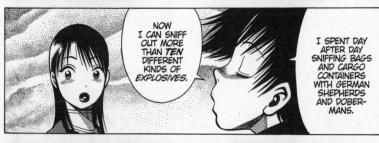

NOW I CAN SNIFF OUT MORE THAN *TEN* DIFFERENT KINDS OF EXPLOSIVES.

I SPENT DAY AFTER DAY SNIFFING BAGS AND CARGO CONTAINERS WITH GERMAN SHEPHERDS AND DOBERMANS.

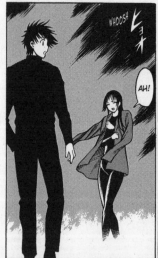

WHOOSH

AH!

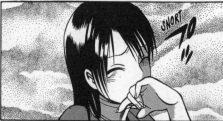

SNORT

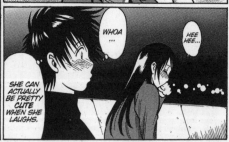

WHOA...

HEE HEE...

SHE CAN ACTUALLY BE PRETTY CUTE WHEN SHE LAUGHS.

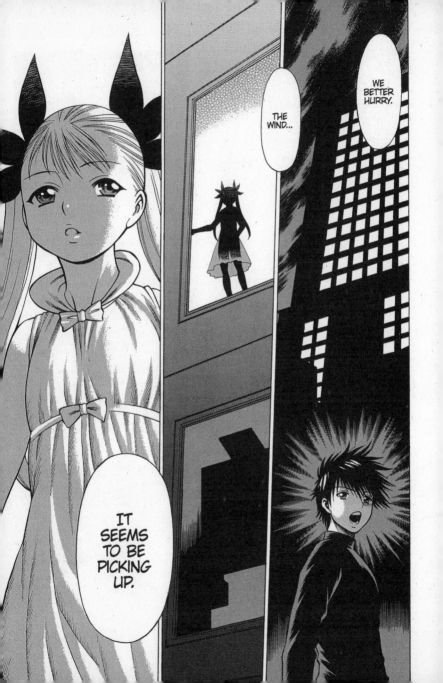

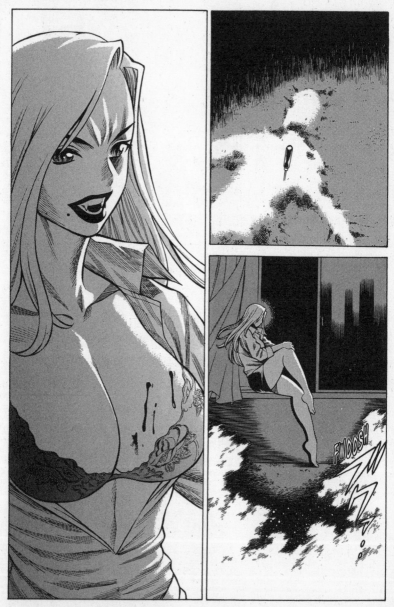

FWOOSH!

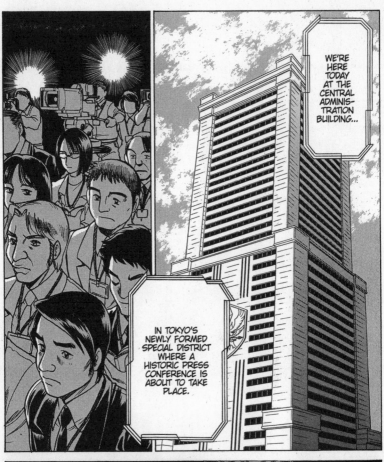

WE'RE HERE TODAY AT THE CENTRAL ADMINISTRATION BUILDING...

IN TOKYO'S NEWLY FORMED SPECIAL DISTRICT WHERE A HISTORIC PRESS CONFERENCE IS ABOUT TO TAKE PLACE.

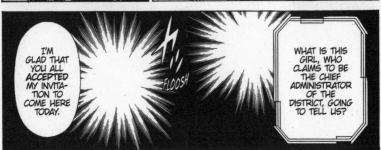

I'M GLAD THAT YOU ALL ACCEPTED MY INVITATION TO COME HERE TODAY.

FLOOSH

WHAT IS THIS GIRL, WHO CLAIMS TO BE THE CHIEF ADMINISTRATOR OF THE DISTRICT, GOING TO TELL US?

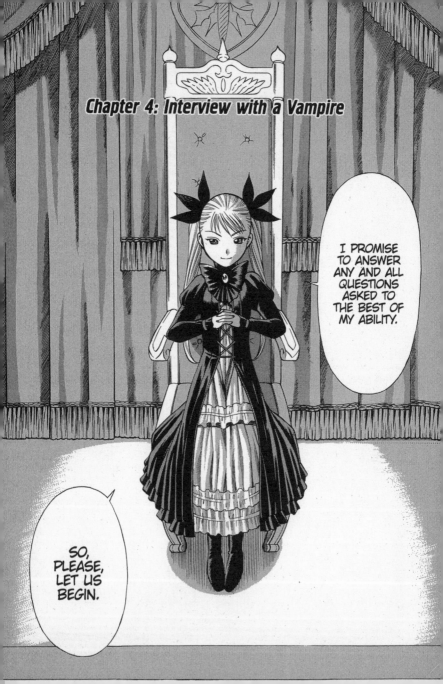

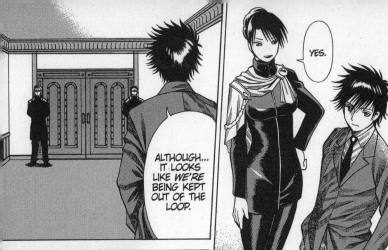

YES.

IT'S STARTED.

ALTHOUGH... IT LOOKS LIKE *WE'RE* BEING KEPT OUT OF THE LOOP.

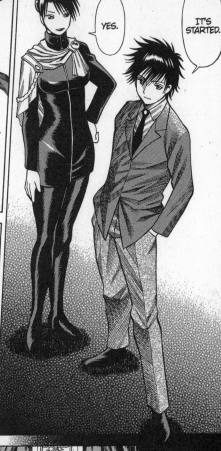

YES, I THOUGHT THAT I COULD AT LEAST NAIL LORD DERMAILLE FOR WHAT HAPPENED THE OTHER DAY...

BUT I UNDER-ESTI-MATED HIM.

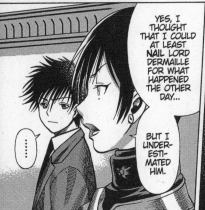

· · · · · ·

THE ASSAILANT WHO ESCAPED VERA'S GRASP WAS INDEED ONE OF THE UNDERLINGS I BROUGHT WITH ME.

3 DAYS AGO...

ACCORD-ING TO MY INVESTIGA-TION...

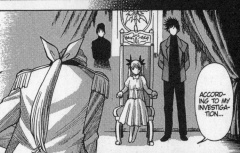

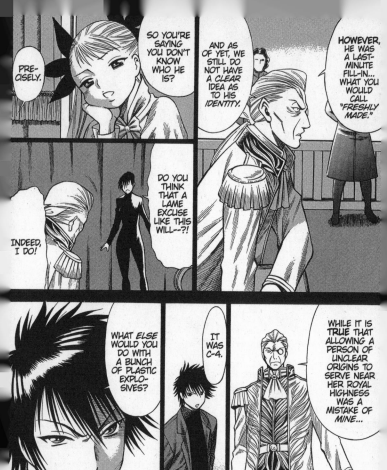

PRECISELY.

SO YOU'RE SAYING YOU DON'T KNOW WHO HE IS?

AND AS OF YET, WE STILL DO NOT HAVE A *CLEAR* IDEA AS TO HIS *IDENTITY.*

HOWEVER, HE WAS A LAST-MINUTE FILL-IN... WHAT YOU WOULD CALL "FRESHLY MADE."

INDEED, I DO!

DO YOU THINK THAT A LAME EXCUSE LIKE THIS WILL--?!

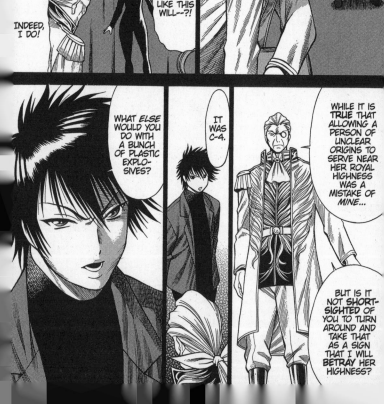

WHAT *ELSE* WOULD YOU DO WITH A BUNCH OF PLASTIC EXPLOSIVES?

IT WAS C-4.

WHILE IT IS *TRUE* THAT ALLOWING A PERSON OF UNCLEAR ORIGINS TO SERVE NEAR HER ROYAL HIGHNESS WAS A MISTAKE OF *MINE...*

BUT IS IT NOT **SHORT-SIGHTED** OF YOU TO TURN AROUND AND TAKE THAT AS A SIGN THAT I WILL **BETRAY** HER HIGHNESS?

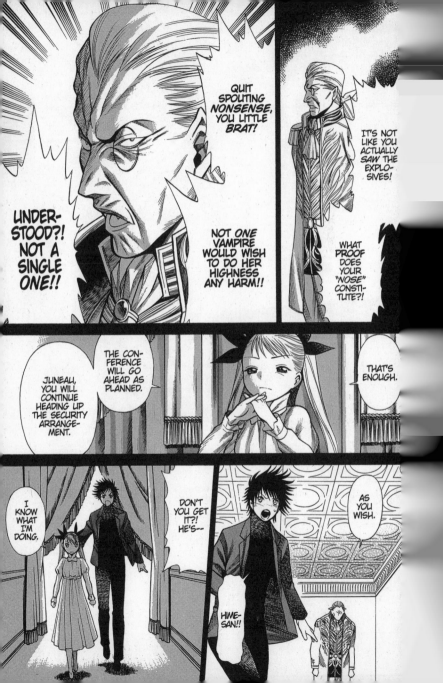

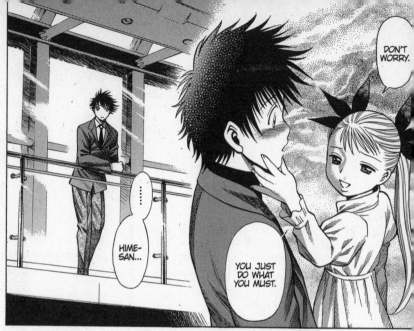

DON'T WORRY.

......

HIME-SAN...

YOU JUST DO WHAT YOU MUST.

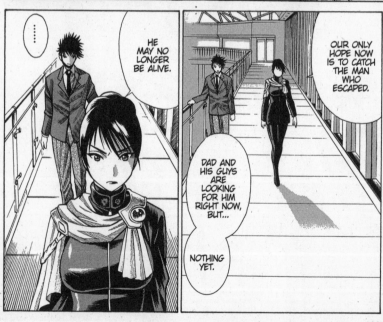

......

HE MAY NO LONGER BE ALIVE.

OUR ONLY HOPE NOW IS TO CATCH THE MAN WHO ESCAPED.

DAD AND HIS GUYS ARE LOOKING FOR HIM RIGHT NOW, BUT...

NOTHING YET.

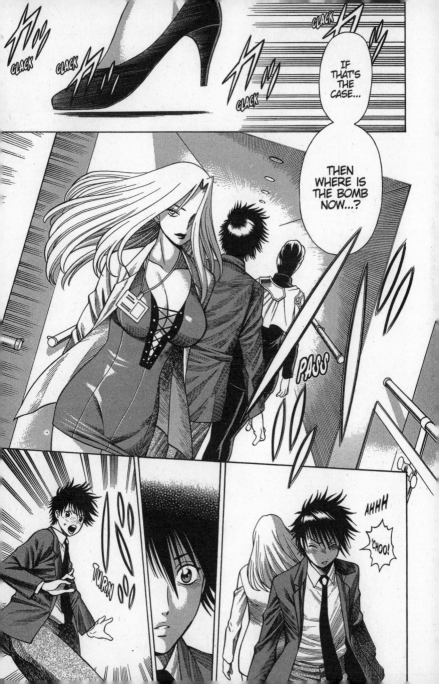

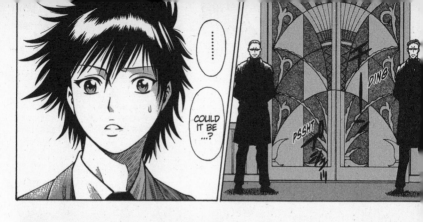

....

COULD IT BE ...?

PSSHT

DING

WELL THEN...

I'D LIKE TO REPRESENT ALL THE ASSEMBLED NEWS CORPORATIONS AND ASK YOU THE FIRST QUESTION.

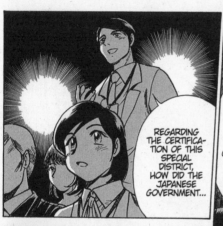

REGARDING THE CERTIFICATION OF THIS SPECIAL DISTRICT, HOW DID THE JAPANESE GOVERNMENT...

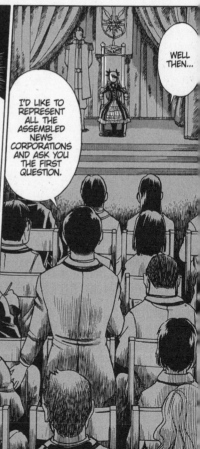

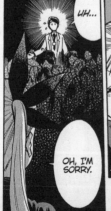

UH...

OH, I'M SORRY.

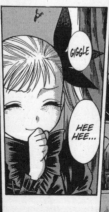

GIGGLE

HEE HEE...

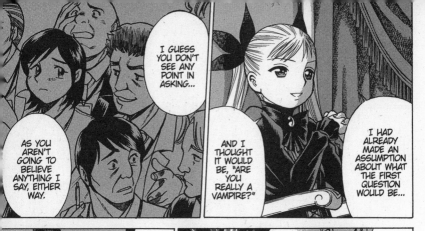

I GUESS YOU DON'T SEE ANY POINT IN ASKING...

AS YOU AREN'T GOING TO BELIEVE ANYTHING I SAY, EITHER WAY.

AND I THOUGHT IT WOULD BE, "ARE YOU REALLY A VAMPIRE?"

I HAD ALREADY MADE AN ASSUMPTION ABOUT WHAT THE FIRST QUESTION WOULD BE...

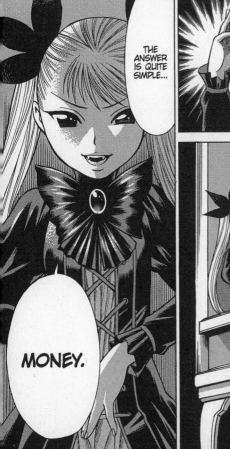

THE ANSWER IS QUITE SIMPLE...

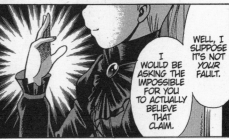

I WOULD BE ASKING THE IMPOSSIBLE FOR YOU TO ACTUALLY BELIEVE THAT CLAIM.

WELL, I SUPPOSE IT'S NOT *YOUR* FAULT.

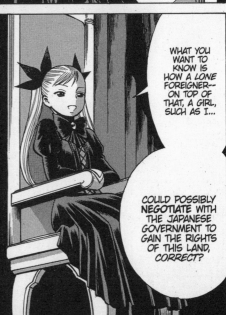

WHAT YOU WANT TO KNOW IS HOW A LONE FOREIGNER-- ON TOP OF THAT, A GIRL, SUCH AS I...

COULD POSSIBLY NEGOTIATE WITH THE JAPANESE GOVERNMENT TO GAIN THE RIGHTS OF THIS LAND, CORRECT?

MONEY.

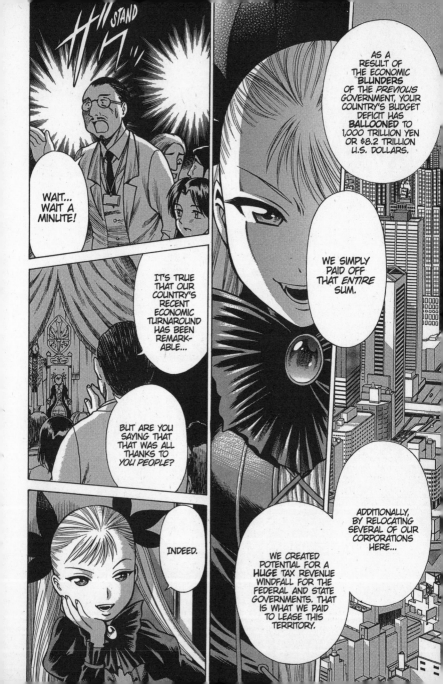

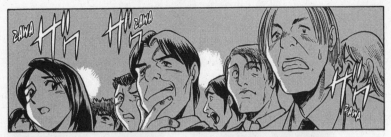

UM... YES...

YOU JUST MENTIONED *LEASING* THIS TERRITORY...

WOULD THAT BE SIMILAR TO PREVIOUS ARRANGEMENTS SUCH AS IN HONG KONG OR MACAU...?

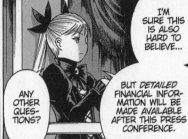

ANY OTHER QUESTIONS?

I'M SURE THIS IS ALSO HARD TO BELIEVE...

BUT *DETAILED* FINANCIAL INFORMATION WILL BE MADE AVAILABLE AFTER THIS PRESS CONFERENCE.

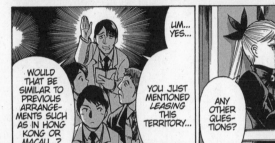

SETTLEMENTS...

SUCH AS HONG KONG AND SHANGHAI WERE IN THE PAST?

YES...A TERRITORY WHICH IS *WITHIN* A COUNTRY BUT *NOT* PART OF THAT COUNTRY.

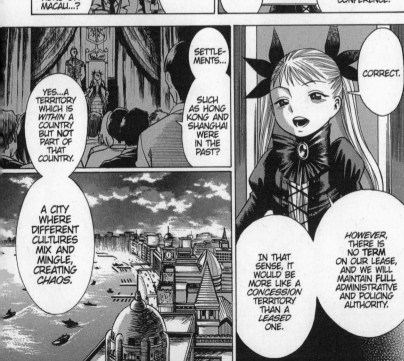

A CITY WHERE DIFFERENT CULTURES MIX AND MINGLE, CREATING CHAOS.

IN THAT SENSE, IT WOULD BE MORE LIKE A *CONCESSION* TERRITORY THAN A *LEASED* ONE.

CORRECT.

HOWEVER, THERE IS NO *TERM* ON OUR LEASE, AND WE WILL MAINTAIN *FULL* ADMINISTRATIVE AND POLICING AUTHORITY.

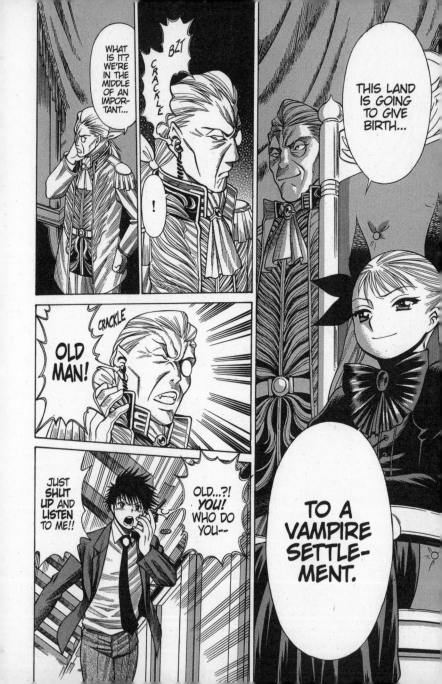

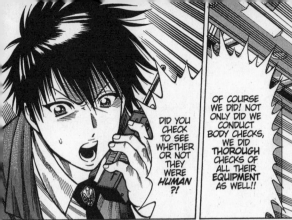
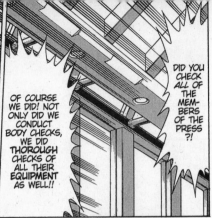

DID YOU CHECK TO SEE WHETHER OR NOT THEY WERE **HUMAN**?!

OF COURSE WE DID! NOT ONLY DID WE CONDUCT BODY CHECKS, WE DID **THOROUGH** CHECKS OF ALL THEIR **EQUIPMENT** AS WELL!!

DID YOU CHECK ALL OF THE MEM-BERS OF THE PRESS?!

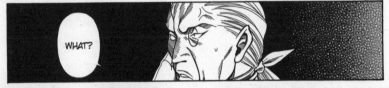

WHAT?

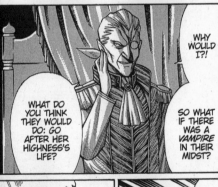
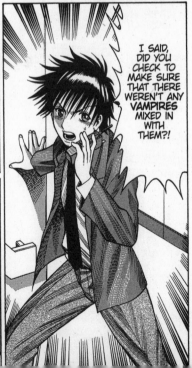

WHY WOULD I?!

WHAT DO YOU THINK THEY WOULD DO: GO AFTER HER HIGHNESS'S LIFE?

SO WHAT IF THERE WAS A **VAMPIRE** IN THEIR MIDST?

I SAID, DID YOU CHECK TO MAKE SURE THAT THERE WEREN'T ANY **VAMPIRES** MIXED IN WITH THEM?!

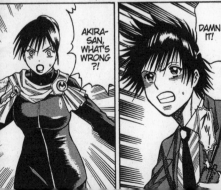

AKIRA-SAN, WHAT'S WRONG?!

DAMN IT!

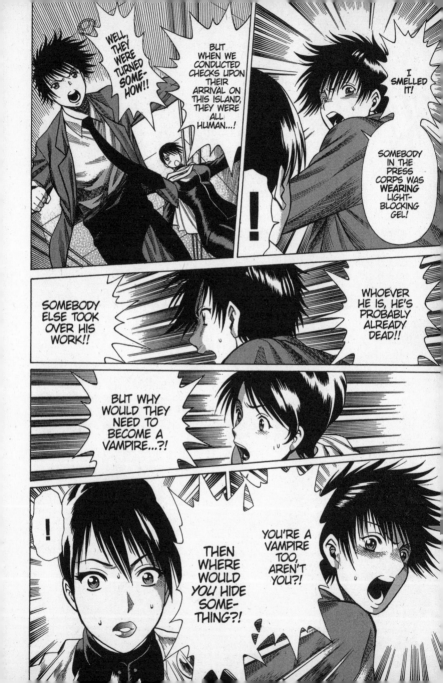

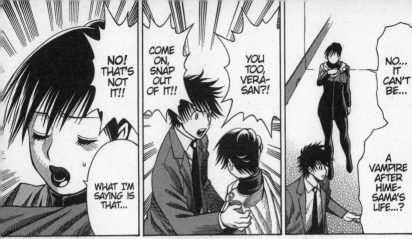

NO! THAT'S NOT IT!!

WHAT I'M SAYING IS THAT...

COME ON, SNAP OUT OF IT!!

YOU TOO, VERA-SAN?!

NO... IT... CAN'T BE...

A VAMPIRE AFTER HIME-SAMA'S LIFE...?

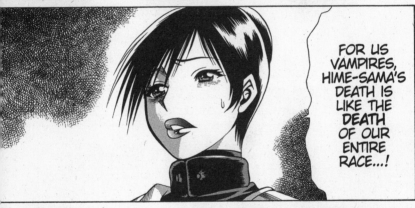

FOR US VAMPIRES, HIME-SAMA'S DEATH IS LIKE THE DEATH OF OUR ENTIRE RACE...!

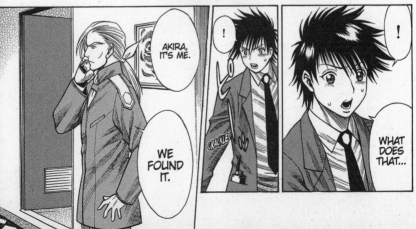

AKIRA, IT'S ME.

WE FOUND IT.

!

!

CRACKLE

WHAT DOES THAT...

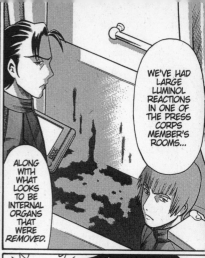

WE'VE HAD LARGE LUMINOL REACTIONS IN ONE OF THE PRESS CORPS MEMBER'S ROOMS...

ALONG WITH WHAT LOOKS TO BE INTERNAL ORGANS THAT WERE REMOVED.

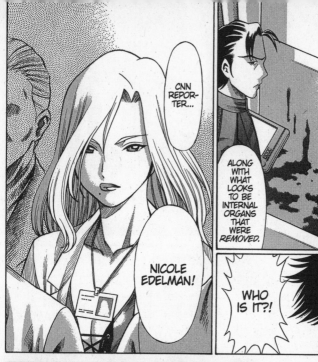

CNN REPORTER...

NICOLE EDELMAN!

WHO IS IT?!

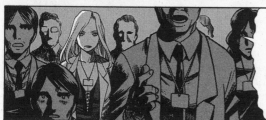

PARDON ME, BUT I CAN'T BELIEVE YOU WOULD HAVE THE FINANCIAL BACKING TO PAY OFF A 1,000 TRILLION YEN DEBT! IT JUST SEEMS HIGHLY **UNLIKELY**!

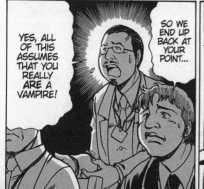

YES, ALL OF THIS ASSUMES THAT YOU REALLY ARE A VAMPIRE!

SO WE END UP BACK AT YOUR POINT...

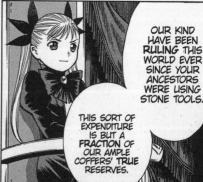

OUR KIND HAVE BEEN **RULING** THIS WORLD EVER SINCE YOUR ANCESTORS WERE USING STONE TOOLS.

THIS SORT OF EXPENDITURE IS BUT A FRACTION OF OUR AMPLE COFFERS' TRUE RESERVES.

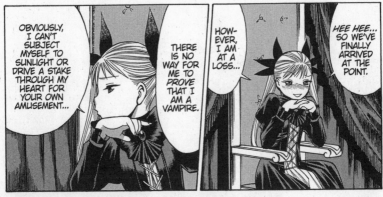

OBVIOUSLY, I CAN'T SUBJECT MYSELF TO SUNLIGHT OR DRIVE A STAKE THROUGH MY HEART FOR YOUR OWN AMUSEMENT...

THERE IS NO WAY FOR ME TO *PROVE* THAT I AM A VAMPIRE.

HOW-EVER, I AM AT A LOSS...

HEE HEE... SO WE'VE FINALLY ARRIVED AT THE POINT.

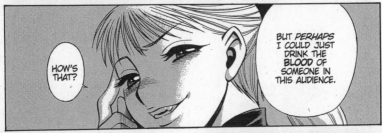

HOW'S THAT?

BUT *PERHAPS* I COULD JUST DRINK THE BLOOD OF SOMEONE IN THIS AUDIENCE.

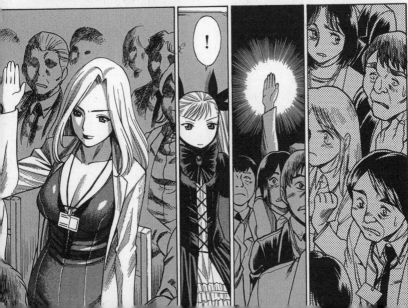

!

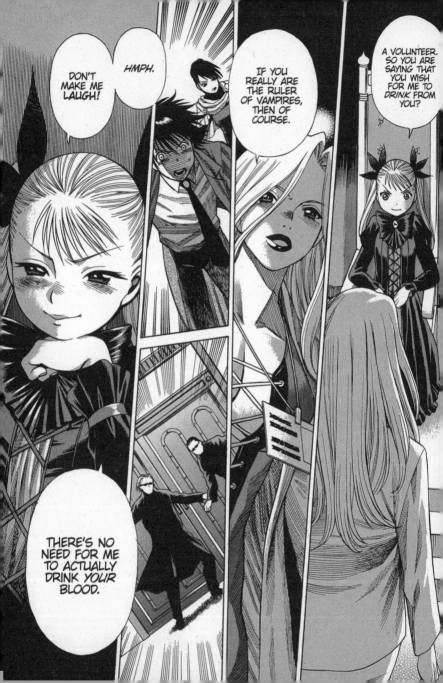

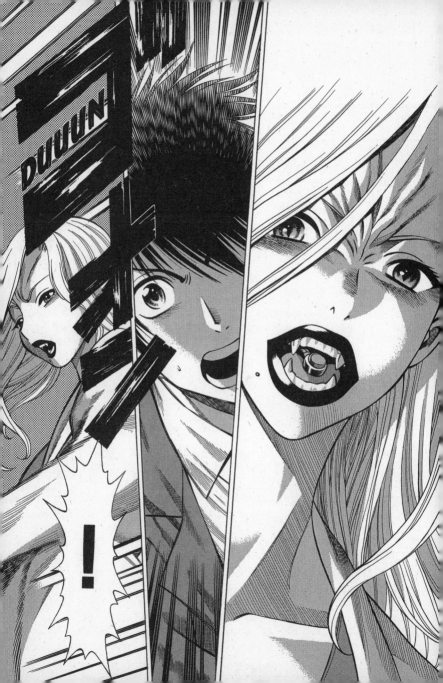

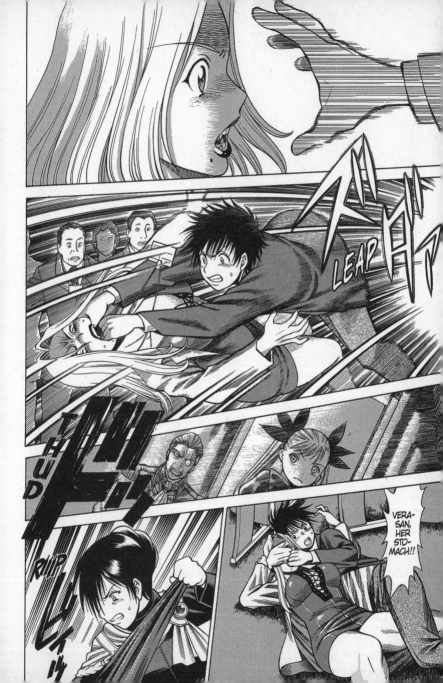

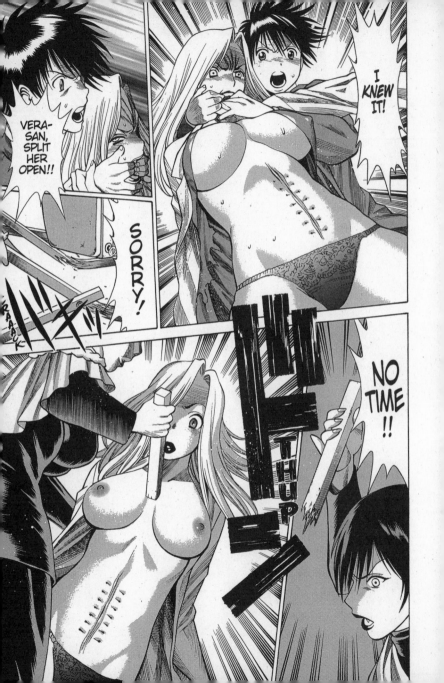

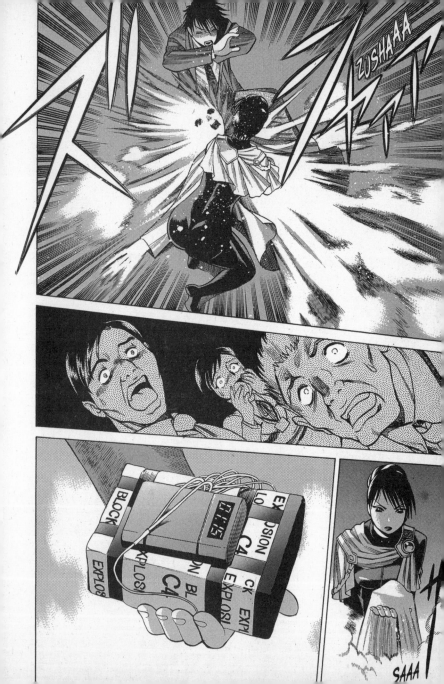

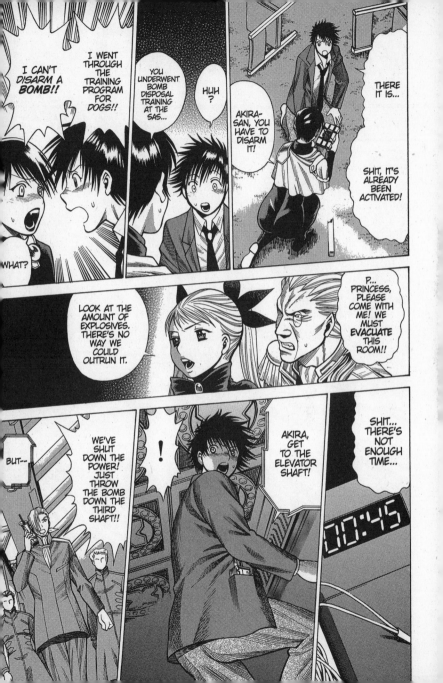

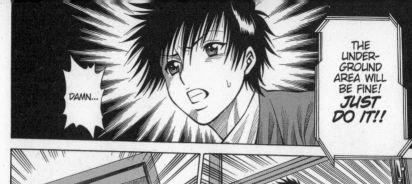

THE UNDER-GROUND AREA WILL BE FINE! **JUST DO IT!!**

DAMN...

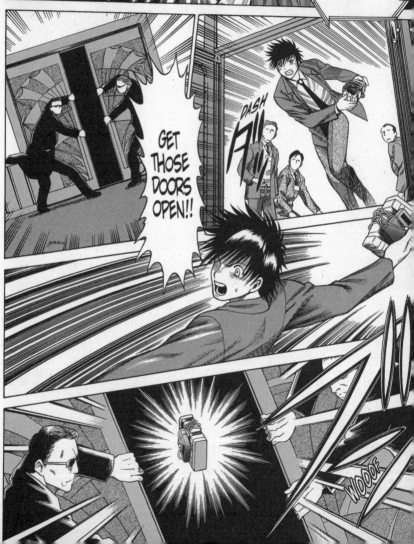

GET THOSE DOORS OPEN!!

DASH

WOOOF

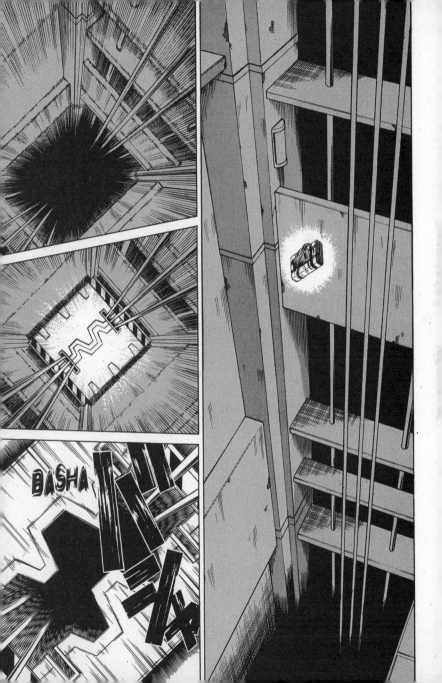

BASHA

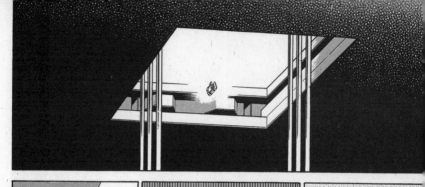

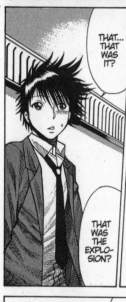

THAT... THAT WAS IT?

THAT WAS THE EXPLO-SION?

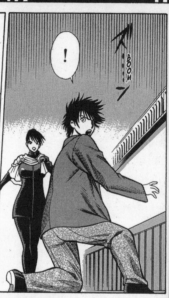

!

BOOM

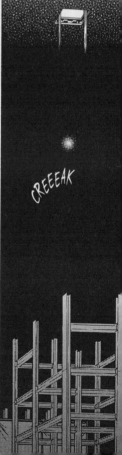

CREEEAK

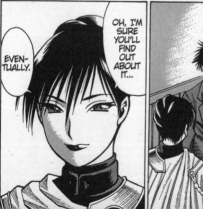

EVEN-TUALLY.

OH, I'M SURE YOU'LL FIND OUT ABOUT IT...

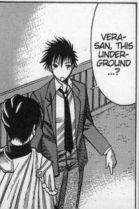

VERA-SAN, THIS UNDER-GROUND...?

IRONICALLY, THAT ENDED UP PROVING THE EXISTENCE OF VAMPIRES.

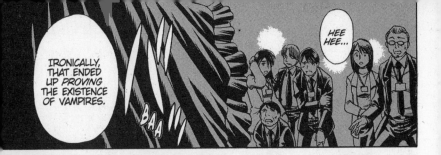

HEE HEE...

BAA

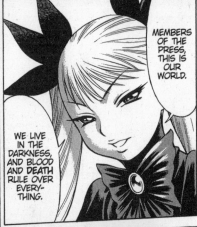

MEMBERS OF THE PRESS, THIS IS OUR WORLD.

WE LIVE IN THE DARKNESS, AND BLOOD AND DEATH RULE OVER EVERY- THING.

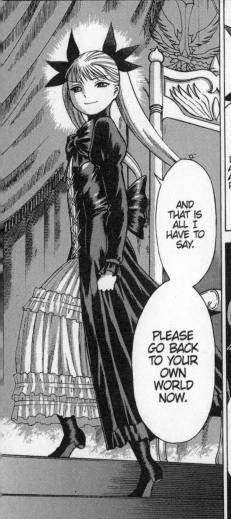

AND THAT IS ALL I HAVE TO SAY.

PLEASE GO BACK TO YOUR OWN WORLD NOW.

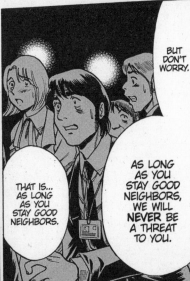

BUT DON'T WORRY.

AS LONG AS YOU STAY GOOD NEIGHBORS, WE WILL NEVER BE A THREAT TO YOU.

THAT IS... AS LONG AS YOU STAY GOOD NEIGHBORS.

IT IS NOW QUITE APPARENT THAT SOMEONE WHO *OPPOSES* YOU, YOUR HIGHNESS, HAS INFILTRATED MY TROOPS.

WELL, JUNEALI...

IF YOU HAVE ANYTHING TO SAY, LET'S HEAR IT.

THEREFORE, I HAVE ORDERED THE EXECUTION OF *EVERY* TROOP MEMBER I BROUGHT WITH ME HERE, TO ELIMINATE THE *ROOT* OF THE EVIL.

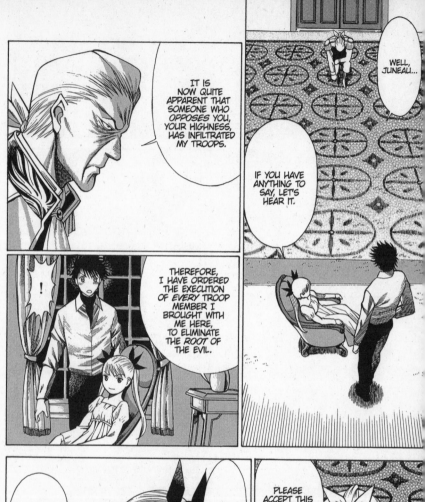

YOU MAY GO NOW.

VERY WELL.

PLEASE ACCEPT THIS AS PROOF OF MY *LOYALTY* TO YOU, YOUR HIGHNESS.

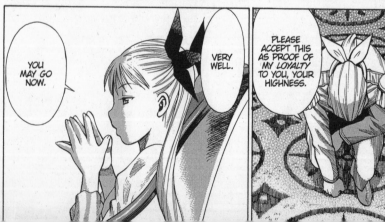

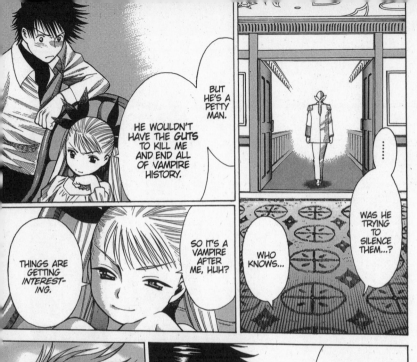

BUT HE'S A PETTY MAN.

HE WOULDN'T HAVE THE GUTS TO KILL ME AND END ALL OF VAMPIRE HISTORY.

......

WAS HE TRYING TO SILENCE THEM...?

WHO KNOWS...

SO IT'S A VAMPIRE AFTER ME, HUH?

THINGS ARE GETTING INTERESTING.

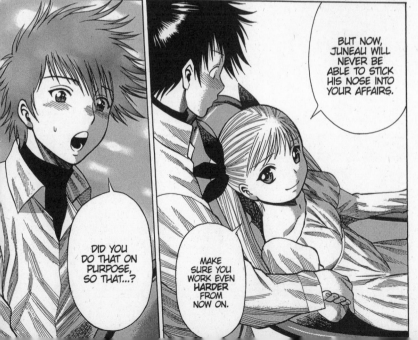

BUT NOW, JUNEAU WILL NEVER BE ABLE TO STICK HIS NOSE INTO YOUR AFFAIRS.

DID YOU DO THAT ON PURPOSE, SO THAT...?

MAKE SURE YOU WORK EVEN HARDER FROM NOW ON.

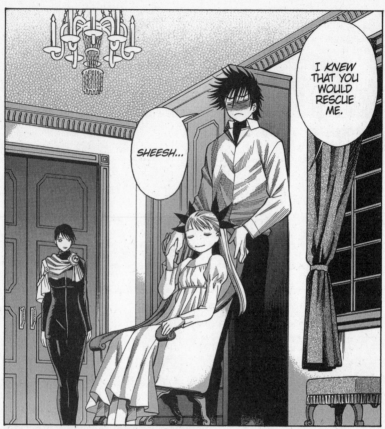

SHEESH...

I *KNEW* THAT YOU WOULD RESCUE ME.

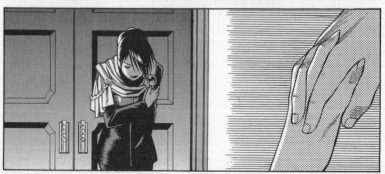

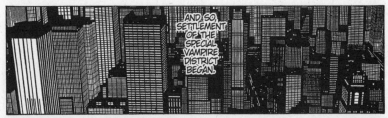

AND SO, SETTLEMENT OF THE SPECIAL VAMPIRE DISTRICT BEGAN.

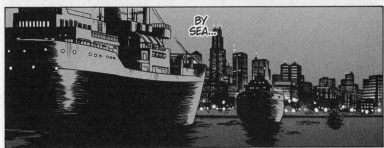

BY SEA...

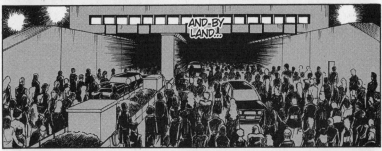

AND BY LAND...

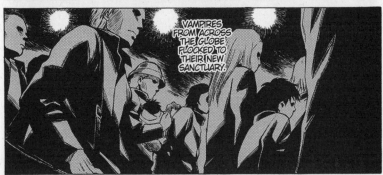

VAMPIRES FROM ACROSS THE GLOBE FLOCKED TO THEIR NEW SANCTUARY.

Chapter 5: On the Night of the Carnival

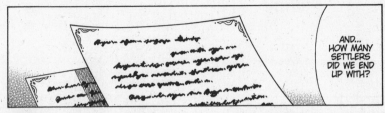

AND... HOW MANY SETTLERS DID WE END UP WITH?

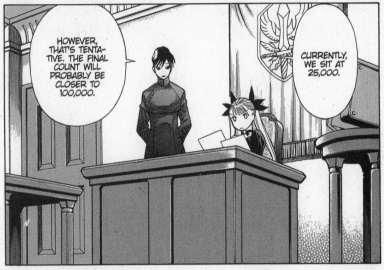

HOWEVER, THAT'S TENTATIVE. THE FINAL COUNT WILL PROBABLY BE CLOSER TO 100,000.

CURRENTLY, WE SIT AT 25,000.

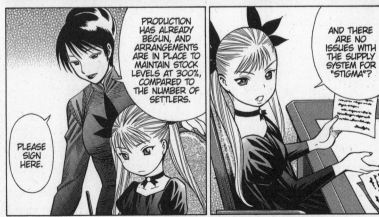

PRODUCTION HAS ALREADY BEGUN, AND ARRANGEMENTS ARE IN PLACE TO MAINTAIN STOCK LEVELS AT 300%, COMPARED TO THE NUMBER OF SETTLERS.

PLEASE SIGN HERE.

AND THERE ARE NO ISSUES WITH THE SUPPLY SYSTEM FOR "STIGMA"?

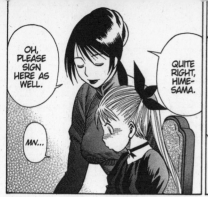

OH, PLEASE SIGN HERE AS WELL.

MN...

QUITE RIGHT, HIME-SAMA.

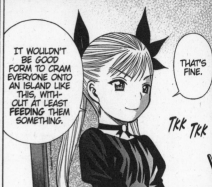

IT WOULDN'T BE GOOD FORM TO CRAM EVERYONE ONTO AN ISLAND LIKE THIS, WITHOUT AT LEAST FEEDING THEM SOMETHING.

THAT'S FINE.

TKK TKK

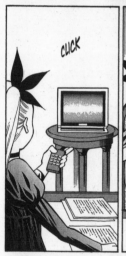

CLICK

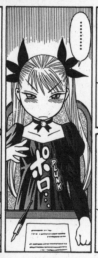

....

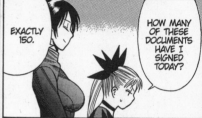

EXACTLY 150.

HOW MANY OF THESE DOCUMENTS HAVE I SIGNED TODAY?

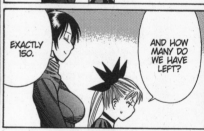

EXACTLY 150.

AND HOW MANY DO WE HAVE LEFT?

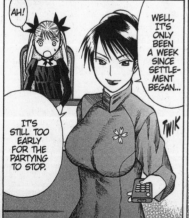

AH!

WELL, IT'S ONLY BEEN A WEEK SINCE SETTLEMENT BEGAN...

IT'S STILL TOO EARLY FOR THE PARTYING TO STOP.

TWIK

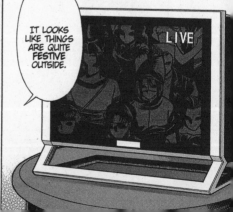

IT LOOKS LIKE THINGS ARE QUITE FESTIVE OUTSIDE.

LIVE

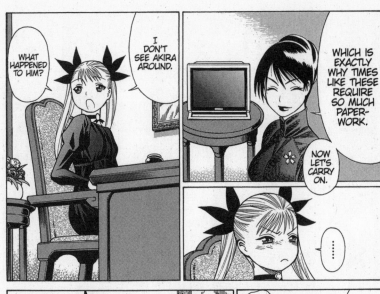

WHAT HAPPENED TO HIM?

I DON'T SEE AKIRA AROUND.

WHICH IS EXACTLY WHY TIMES LIKE THESE REQUIRE SO MUCH PAPERWORK.

NOW LET'S CARRY ON.

......

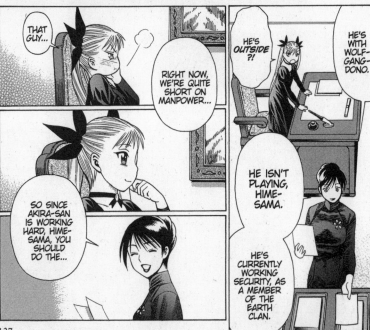

THAT GUY...

RIGHT NOW, WE'RE QUITE SHORT ON MANPOWER...

SO SINCE AKIRA-SAN IS WORKING HARD, HIME-SAMA, YOU SHOULD DO THE...

HE'S OUTSIDE?!

HE'S WITH WOLFGANG-DONO.

HE ISN'T PLAYING, HIME-SAMA.

HE'S CURRENTLY WORKING SECURITY, AS A MEMBER OF THE EARTH CLAN.

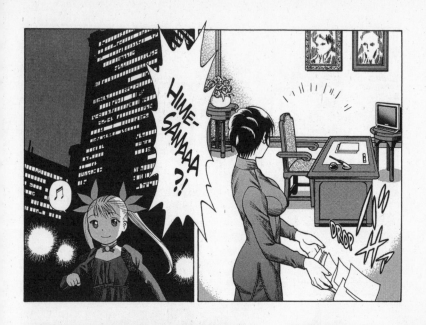

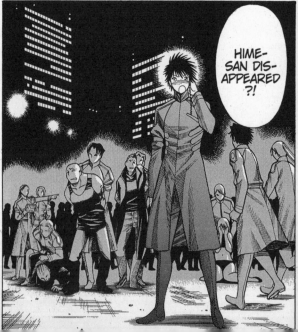

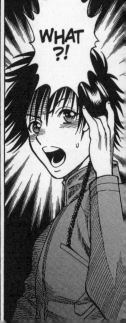

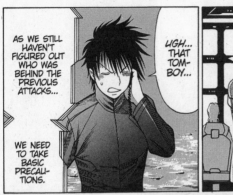

AS WE STILL HAVEN'T FIGURED OUT WHO WAS BEHIND THE PREVIOUS ATTACKS...

UGH... THAT TOM-BOY...

WE NEED TO TAKE BASIC PRECAU-TIONS.

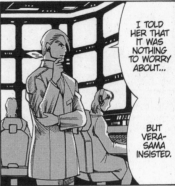

I TOLD HER THAT IT WAS NOTHING TO WORRY ABOUT...

BUT VERA-SAMA INSISTED.

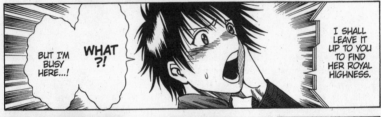

WHAT ?!

BUT I'M BUSY HERE...!

I SHALL LEAVE IT UP TO YOU TO FIND HER ROYAL HIGHNESS.

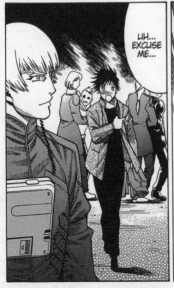

UH... EXCUSE ME...

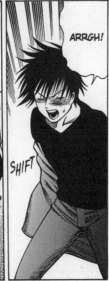

ARRGH!

SHIFT

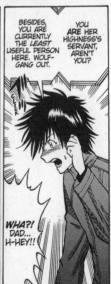

BESIDES, YOU ARE CURRENTLY THE *LEAST* USEFUL PERSON HERE. WOLF-GANG OUT.

YOU ARE HER HIGHNESS'S SERVANT, AREN'T YOU?

WHA?! DAD... H-HEY!!

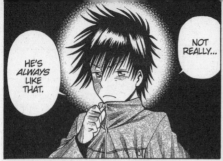

HE'S ALWAYS LIKE THAT.

NOT REALLY...

WE HEARD.

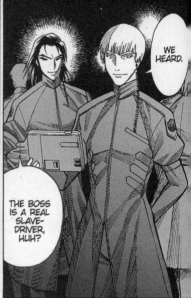

THE BOSS IS A REAL SLAVE-DRIVER, HUH?

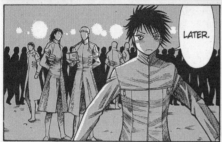

LATER.

YEAH.

THE BOSS CAN SURE BE A PRICK SOMETIMES...

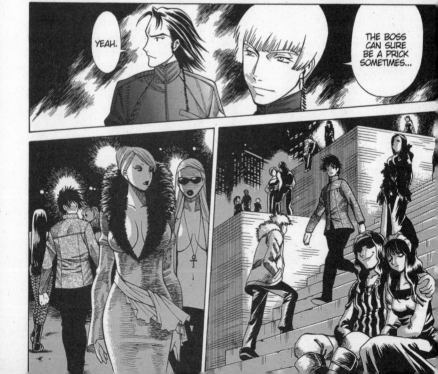

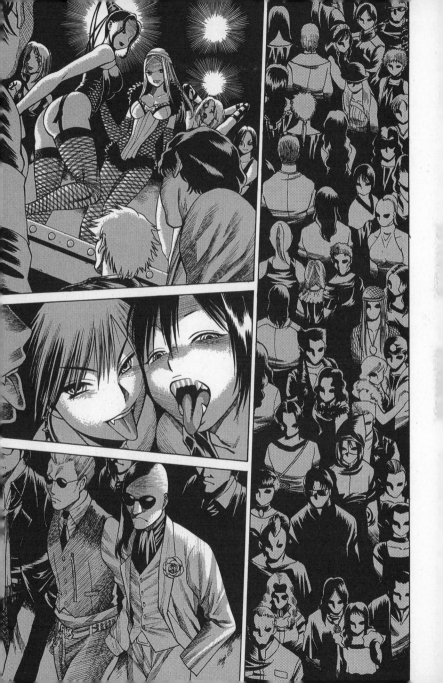

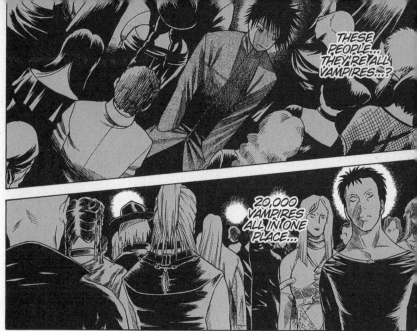

THESE PEOPLE... THEY'RE ALL VAMPIRES...?

20,000 VAMPIRES ALL IN ONE PLACE...

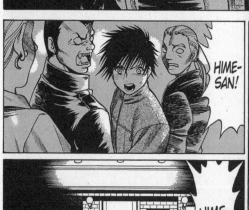

HIME-SAN!

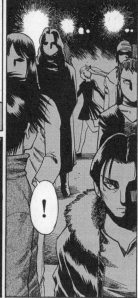

!

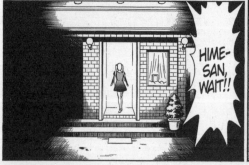

HIME-SAN, WAIT!!

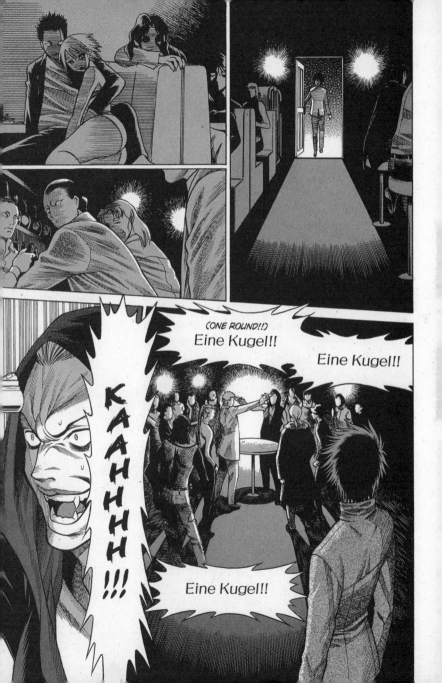

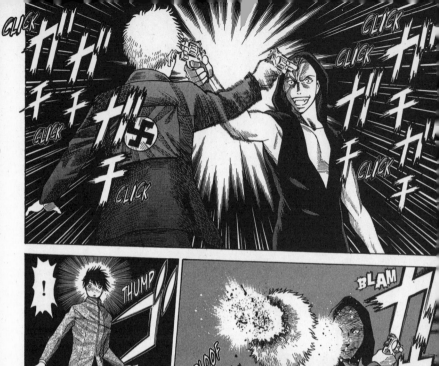

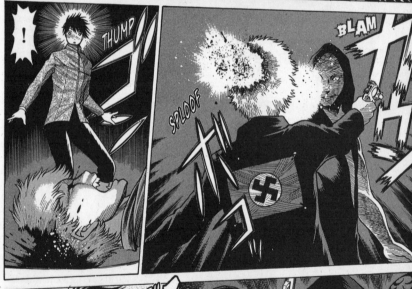

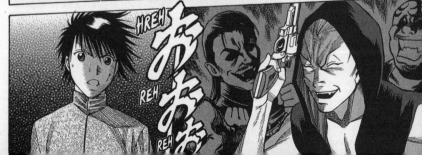

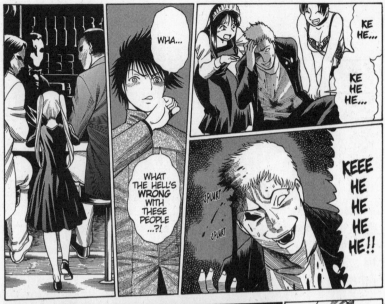

WHA...

WHAT THE HELL'S **WRONG** WITH THESE PEOPLE ...?!

KE HE...

KE HE HE...

SPLURT

SPLURT

KEEE HE HE HE HE!!

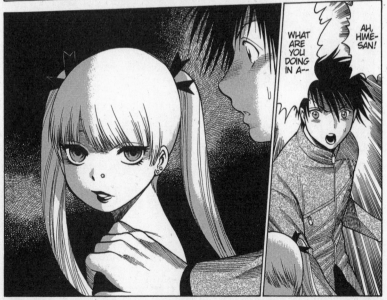

WHAT ARE YOU DOING IN A--

AH, HIME-SAN!

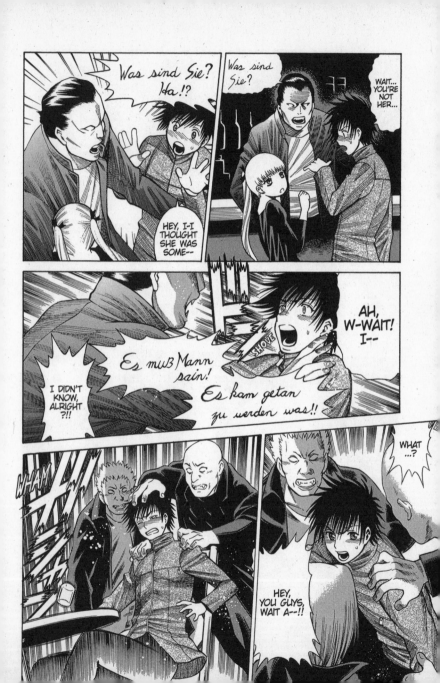

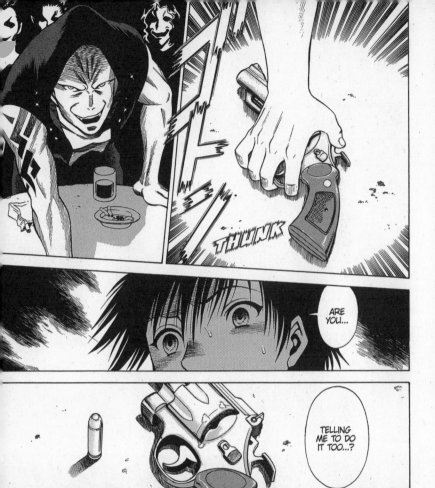

THUNK

ARE YOU...

TELLING ME TO DO IT TOO...?

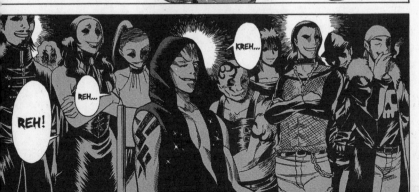

REH!

REH...

KREH...

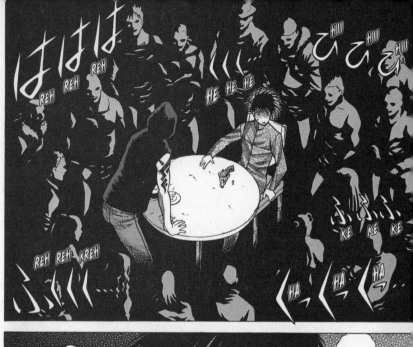

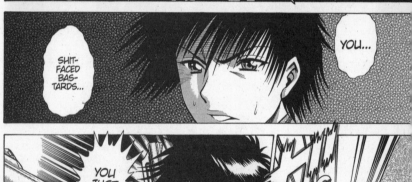

SHIT-FACED BAS-TARDS...

YOU...

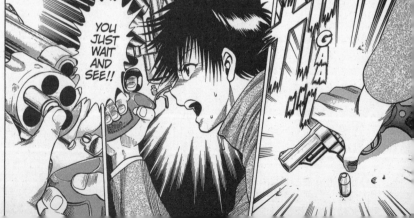

YOU JUST WAIT AND SEE!!

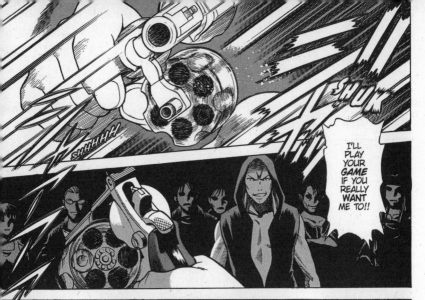

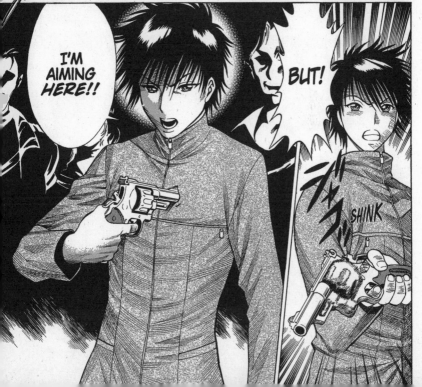

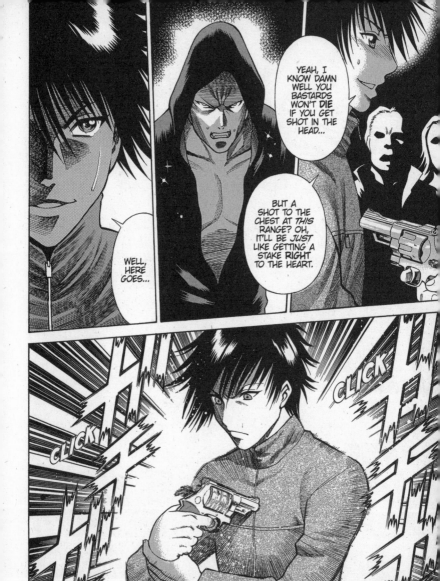

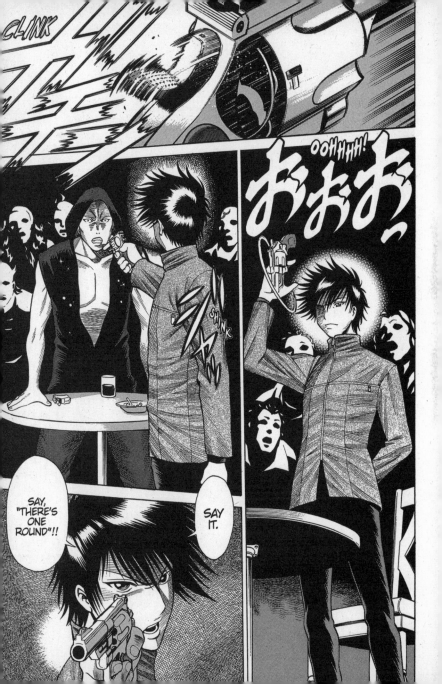

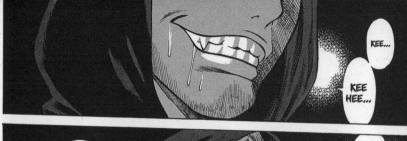

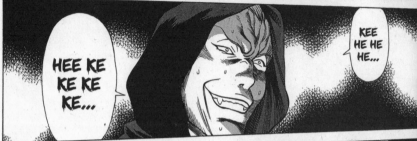

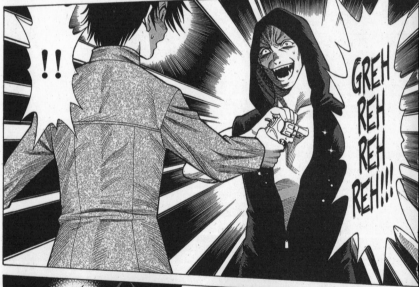

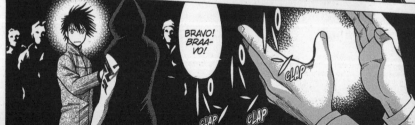

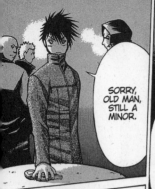

SORRY, OLD MAN, STILL A MINOR.

WHY DON'T YOU JUST IGNORE HIM AND COME OVER HERE?

LET ME BUY YOU A DRINK.

YOU'VE GOT QUITE A BIT OF COURAGE!

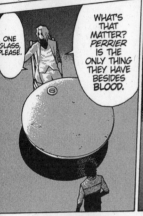

ONE GLASS, PLEASE.

WHAT'S THAT MATTER? *PERRIER* IS THE ONLY THING THEY HAVE BESIDES BLOOD.

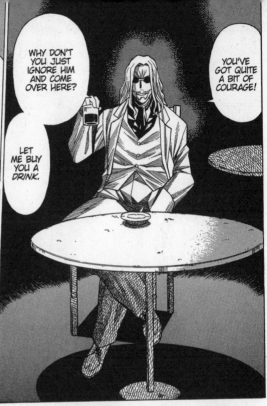

REMARK-ABLE.

IT WOULD SEEM YOUR VISION IS EVEN BETTER THAN THE RUMORS SAY.

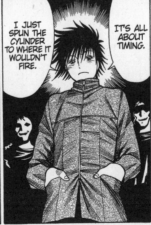

I JUST SPUN THE CYLINDER TO WHERE IT WOULDN'T FIRE.

IT'S ALL ABOUT TIMING.

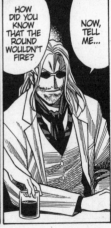

HOW DID YOU KNOW THAT THE ROUND WOULDN'T FIRE?

NOW, TELL ME...

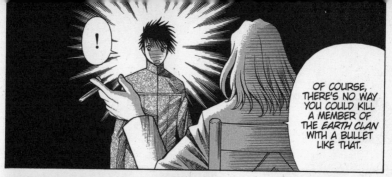

OF COURSE, THERE'S NO WAY YOU COULD KILL A MEMBER OF THE *EARTH CLAN* WITH A BULLET LIKE THAT.

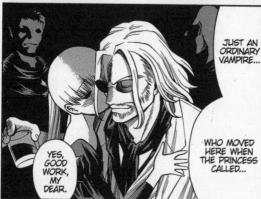

JUST AN ORDINARY VAMPIRE...

WHO MOVED HERE WHEN THE PRINCESS CALLED...

YES, GOOD WORK, MY DEAR.

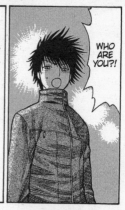

WHO ARE YOU?!

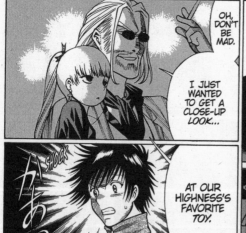

OH, DON'T BE MAD.

I JUST WANTED TO GET A CLOSE-UP LOOK...

AT OUR HIGHNESS'S FAVORITE TOY.

SHOCK

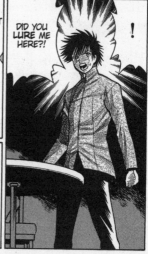

DID YOU LURE ME HERE?!

!

154

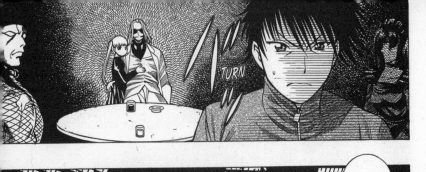

TURN

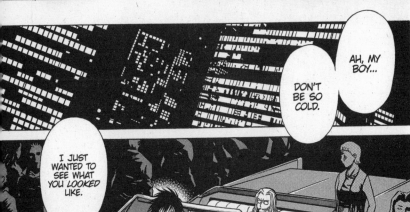

AH, MY BOY...

DON'T BE SO COLD.

I JUST WANTED TO SEE WHAT YOU *LOOKED* LIKE.

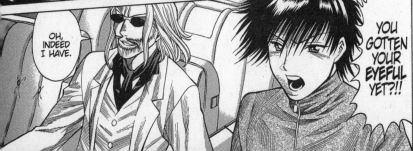

OH, INDEED I HAVE.

YOU GOTTEN YOUR EYEFUL YET?!!

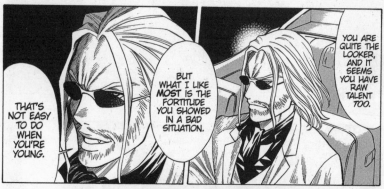

YOU ARE QUITE THE LOOKER, AND IT SEEMS YOU HAVE RAW TALENT TOO.

BUT WHAT I LIKE MOST IS THE FORTITUDE YOU SHOWED IN A BAD SITUATION.

THAT'S NOT EASY TO DO WHEN YOU'RE YOUNG.

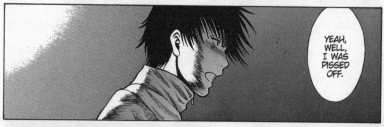

YEAH, WELL, I WAS PISSED OFF.

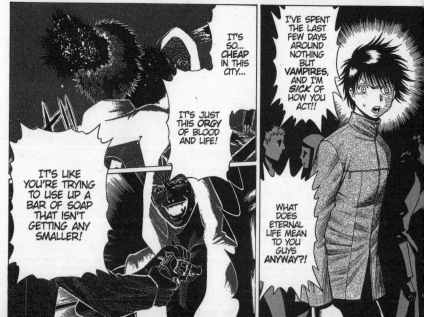

I'VE SPENT THE LAST FEW DAYS AROUND NOTHING BUT VAMPIRES, AND I'M SICK OF HOW YOU ACT!!

IT'S SO... CHEAP IN THIS CITY...

IT'S JUST THIS ORGY OF BLOOD AND LIFE!

IT'S LIKE YOU'RE TRYING TO USE UP A BAR OF SOAP THAT ISN'T GETTING ANY SMALLER!

WHAT DOES ETERNAL LIFE MEAN TO YOU GUYS ANYWAY?!

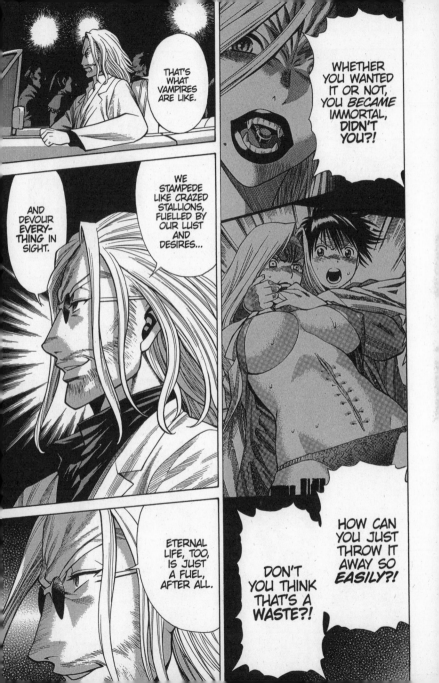

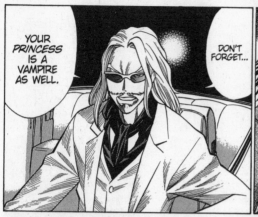

YOUR *PRINCESS* IS A VAMPIRE AS WELL.

DON'T FORGET...

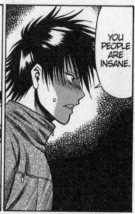

YOU PEOPLE ARE INSANE.

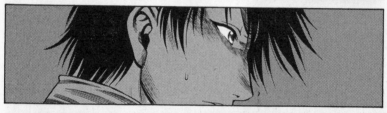

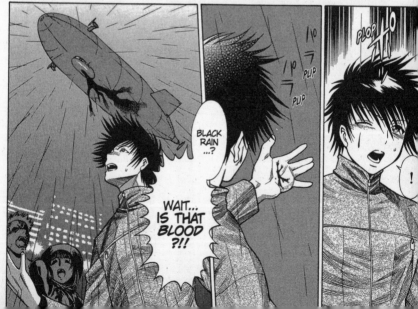

BLACK RAIN ...?

PLIP

PLIP

PLOP

WAIT... IS THAT *BLOOD* ?!!

!

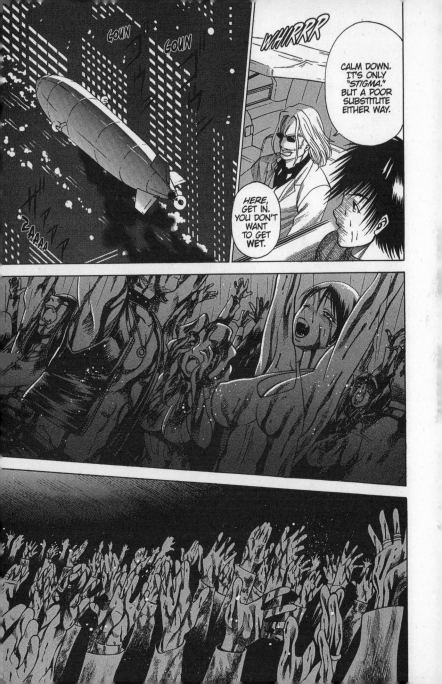

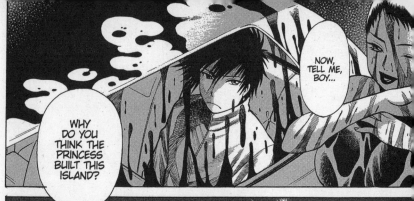

NOW, TELL ME, BOY...

WHY DO YOU THINK THE PRINCESS BUILT THIS ISLAND?

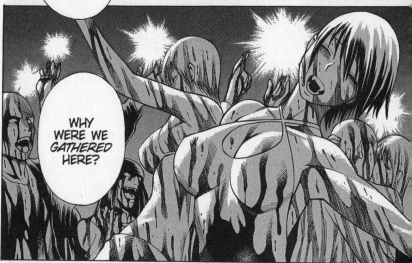

WHY WERE WE GATHERED HERE?

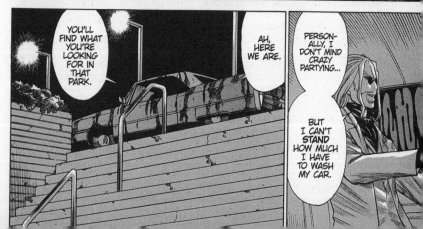

YOU'LL FIND WHAT YOU'RE LOOKING FOR IN THAT PARK.

AH, HERE WE ARE.

PERSONALLY, I DON'T MIND CRAZY PARTYING...

BUT I CAN'T STAND HOW MUCH I HAVE TO WASH MY CAR.

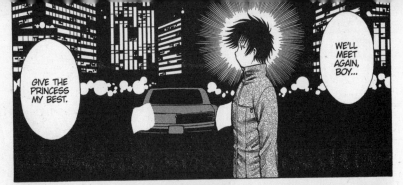

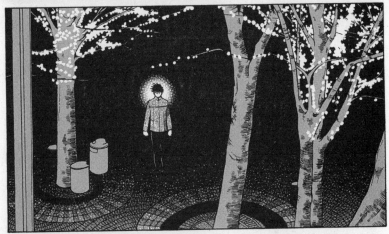

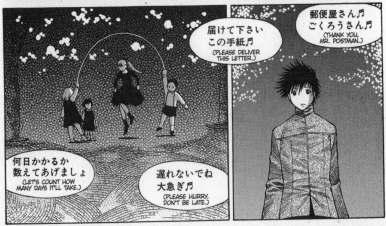

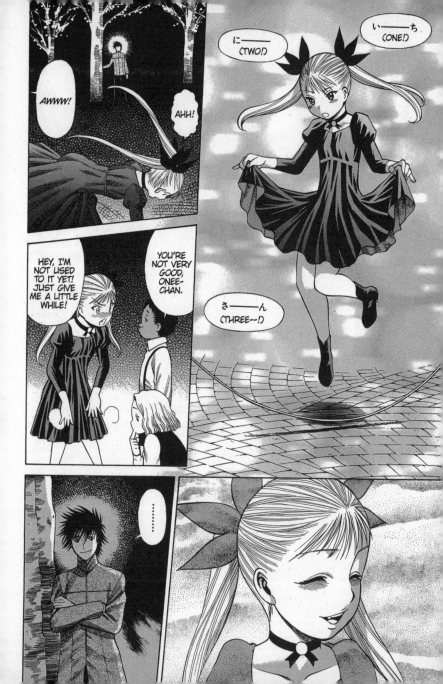

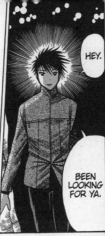

HEY.

BEEN LOOKING FOR YA.

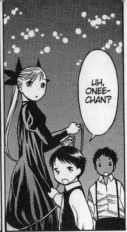

UH, ONEE-CHAN?

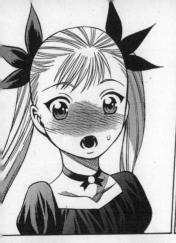

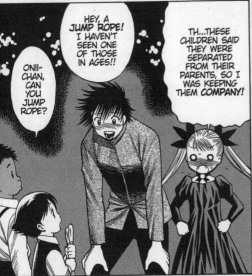

ONII-CHAN, CAN YOU JUMP ROPE?

HEY, A JUMP ROPE! I HAVEN'T SEEN ONE OF THOSE IN AGES!!

TH...THESE CHILDREN SAID THEY WERE SEPARATED FROM THEIR PARENTS, SO I WAS KEEPING THEM COMPANY!

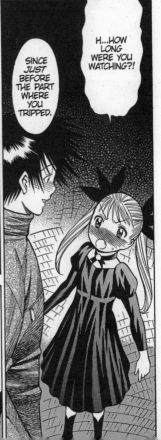

SINCE JUST BEFORE THE PART WHERE YOU TRIPPED.

H...HOW LONG WERE YOU WATCHING?!

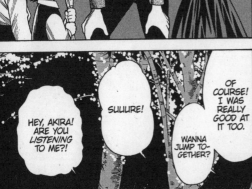

HEY, AKIRA! ARE YOU LISTENING TO ME?!

SUUURE!

WANNA JUMP TO-GETHER?

OF COURSE! I WAS REALLY GOOD AT IT TOO.

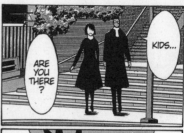

ARE YOU THERE?

KIDS...

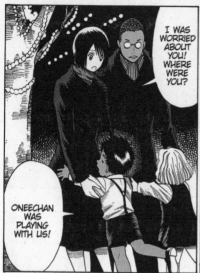

I WAS WORRIED ABOUT YOU! WHERE WERE YOU?

ONEECHAN WAS PLAYING WITH US!

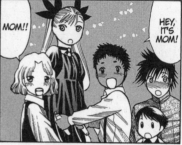

MOM!!

HEY, IT'S MOM!

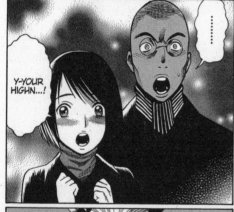

Y-YOUR HIGHN...!

....

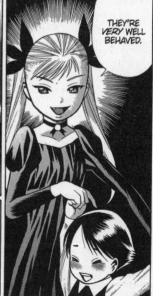

THEY'RE VERY WELL BEHAVED.

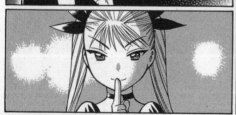

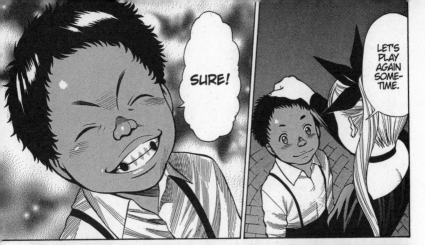

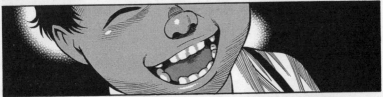

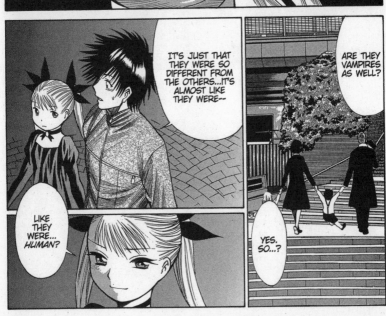

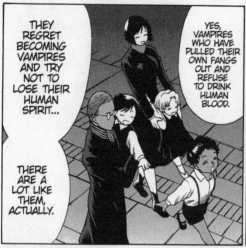

THEY REGRET BECOMING VAMPIRES AND TRY NOT TO LOSE THEIR HUMAN SPIRIT...

THERE ARE A LOT LIKE THEM, ACTUALLY.

YES, VAMPIRES WHO HAVE PULLED THEIR OWN FANGS OUT AND REFUSE TO DRINK HUMAN BLOOD.

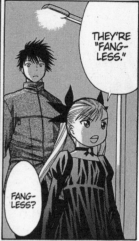

THEY'RE "FANG-LESS."

FANG-LESS?

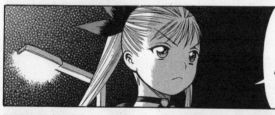

THEY WERE FORCED TO LEAD A LIFE OF EXILE.

AND IT'S BECAUSE OF THIS, THEY WERE PERSECUTED NOT ONLY BY HUMANS BUT OTHER VAMPIRES AS WELL.

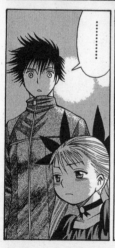

．．．．．．．．

NOW, WE HAVE THE BUND.

AS LONG AS IT'S HERE, THEIR PEACE WILL *NEVER* BE DISTURBED AGAIN.

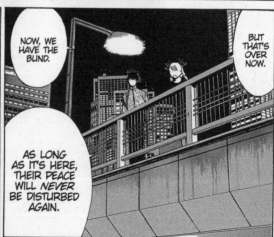

BUT THAT'S OVER NOW.

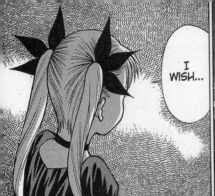

I WISH...

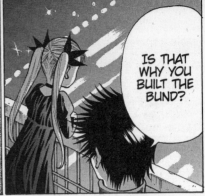

IS THAT WHY YOU BUILT THE BUND?

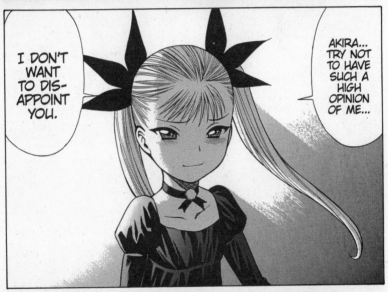

I DON'T WANT TO DIS-APPOINT YOU.

AKIRA... TRY NOT TO HAVE SUCH A HIGH OPINION OF ME...

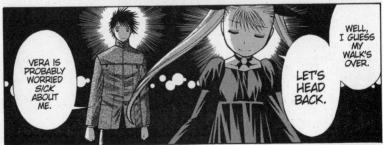

VERA IS PROBABLY WORRIED SICK ABOUT ME.

WELL, I GUESS MY WALK'S OVER.

LET'S HEAD BACK.

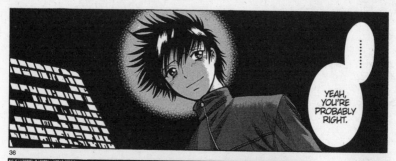

YEAH, YOU'RE PROBABLY RIGHT.

36

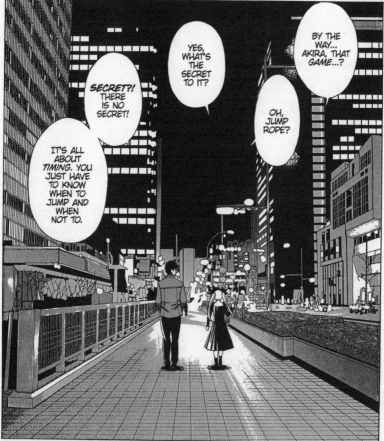

BY THE WAY... AKIRA, THAT GAME...?

YES, WHAT'S THE SECRET TO IT?

OH, JUMP ROPE?

SECRET?! THERE IS NO SECRET!

IT'S ALL ABOUT TIMING. YOU JUST HAVE TO KNOW WHEN TO JUMP AND WHEN NOT TO.

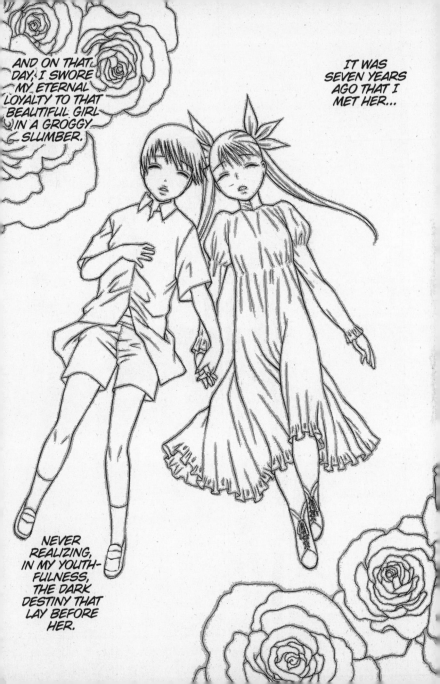

AND ON THAT DAY, I SWORE MY ETERNAL LOYALTY TO THAT BEAUTIFUL GIRL IN A GROGGY SLUMBER.

IT WAS SEVEN YEARS AGO THAT I MET HER...

NEVER REALIZING, IN MY YOUTHFULNESS, THE DARK DESTINY THAT LAY BEFORE HER.

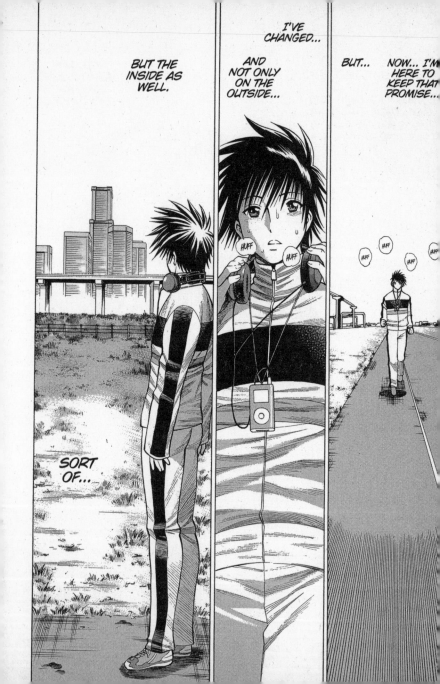

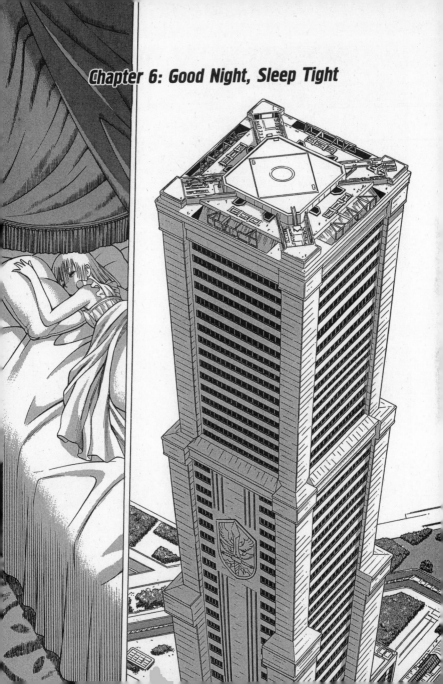

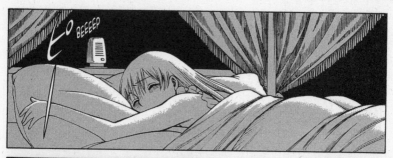

BEEEEP

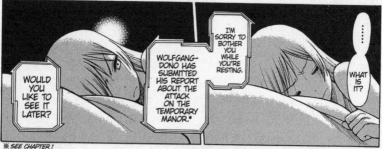

WOULD YOU LIKE TO SEE IT LATER?

WOLFGANG-DONO HAS SUBMITTED HIS REPORT ABOUT THE ATTACK ON THE TEMPORARY MANOR.*

I'M SORRY TO BOTHER YOU WHILE YOU'RE RESTING.

......

WHAT IS IT?

※ SEE CHAPTER 1

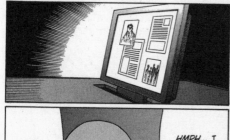

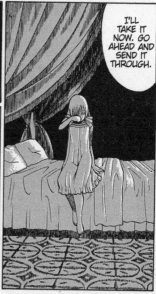

I'LL TAKE IT NOW. GO AHEAD AND SEND IT THROUGH.

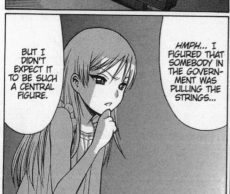

BUT I DIDN'T EXPECT IT TO BE SUCH A CENTRAL FIGURE.

HMPH... I FIGURED THAT SOMEBODY IN THE GOVERN-MENT WAS PULLING THE STRINGS...

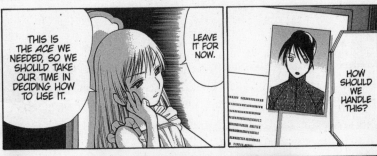

THIS IS THE *ACE* WE NEEDED, SO WE SHOULD TAKE OUR TIME IN DECIDING HOW TO USE IT.

LEAVE IT FOR NOW.

HOW SHOULD WE HANDLE THIS?

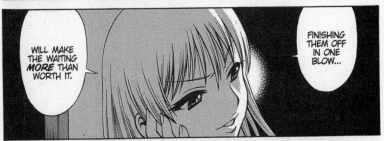

WILL MAKE THE WAITING *MORE* THAN WORTH IT.

FINISHING THEM OFF IN ONE BLOW...

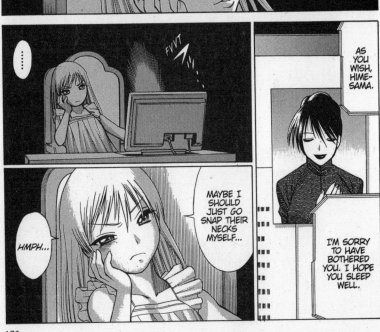

·······

FVVT

AS YOU WISH, HIME-SAMA.

MAYBE I SHOULD JUST GO SNAP THEIR NECKS MYSELF...

HMPH...

I'M SORRY TO HAVE BOTHERED YOU. I HOPE YOU SLEEP WELL.

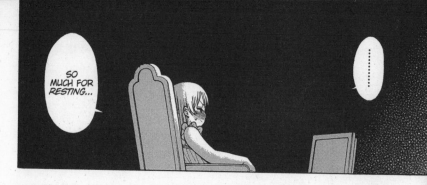

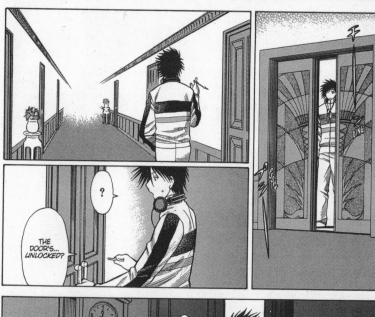

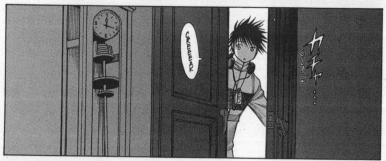

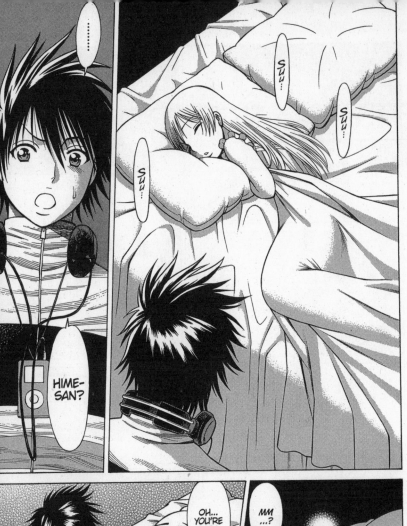

HIME-
SAN?

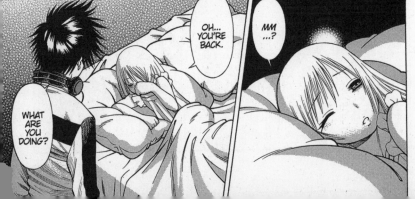

OH....
YOU'RE
BACK.

MM
...?

WHAT
ARE
YOU
DOING?

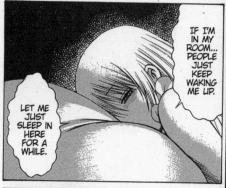

IF I'M IN MY ROOM... PEOPLE JUST KEEP WAKING ME UP.

LET ME JUST SLEEP IN HERE FOR A WHILE.

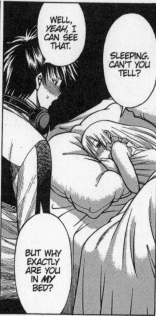

WELL, YEAH, I CAN SEE THAT.

SLEEPING. CAN'T YOU TELL?

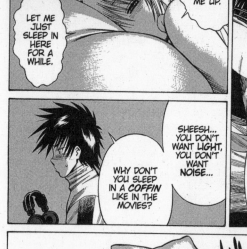

WHY DON'T YOU SLEEP IN A *COFFIN* LIKE IN THE MOVIES?

SHEESH... YOU DON'T WANT *LIGHT*, YOU DON'T WANT *NOISE*...

BUT WHY EXACTLY ARE YOU IN *MY* BED?

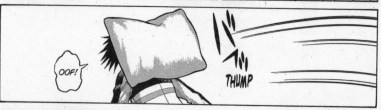

OOF!

THUMP

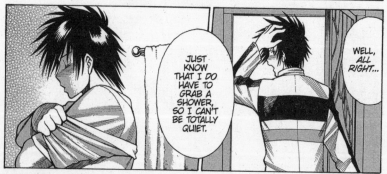

JUST KNOW THAT I DO HAVE TO GRAB A SHOWER, SO I CAN'T BE TOTALLY QUIET.

WELL, ALL RIGHT...

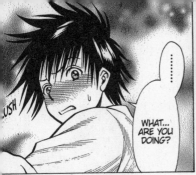

WHAT... ARE YOU DOING?

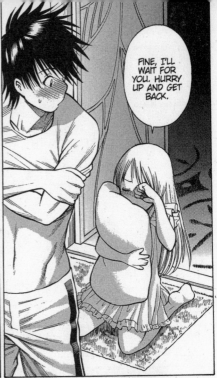

FINE, I'LL WAIT FOR YOU. HURRY UP AND GET BACK.

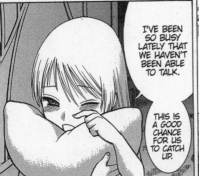

I'VE BEEN SO BUSY LATELY THAT WE HAVEN'T BEEN ABLE TO TALK.

THIS IS A GOOD CHANCE FOR US TO CATCH UP.

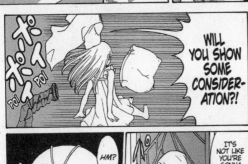

WILL YOU SHOW SOME CONSIDERATION?!

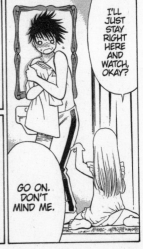

I'LL JUST STAY RIGHT HERE AND WATCH, OKAY?

GO ON. DON'T MIND ME.

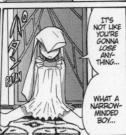

HM?

IT'S NOT LIKE YOU'RE GONNA LOSE ANY- THING...

WHAT A NARROW- MINDED BOY...

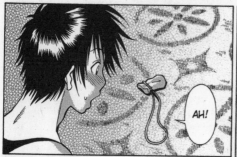

AH!

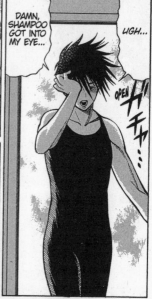

DAMN, SHAMPOO GOT INTO MY EYE...

UGH...

OPEN

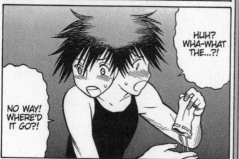

HUH? WHA-WHAT THE...?!

NO WAY! WHERE'D IT GO?!

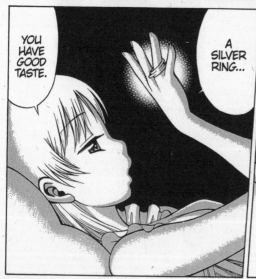

YOU HAVE GOOD TASTE.

A SILVER RING...

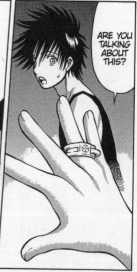

ARE YOU TALKING ABOUT THIS?

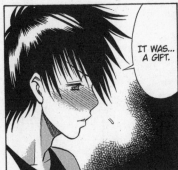

IT WAS... A GIFT.

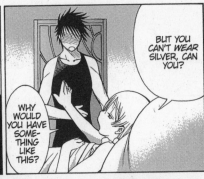

WHY WOULD YOU HAVE SOME-THING LIKE THIS?

BUT YOU CAN'T *WEAR* SILVER, CAN YOU?

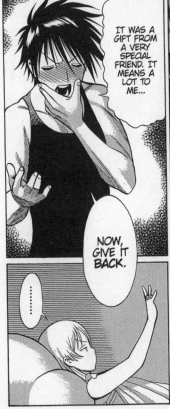

IT WAS A GIFT FROM A VERY SPECIAL FRIEND. IT MEANS A LOT TO ME...

NOW, GIVE IT BACK.

· · · · · · ·

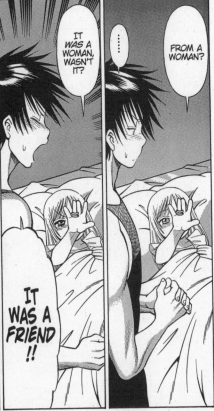

IT *WAS A* WOMAN, WASN'T IT?

· · · ·

FROM A WOMAN?

IT WAS A FRIEND !!

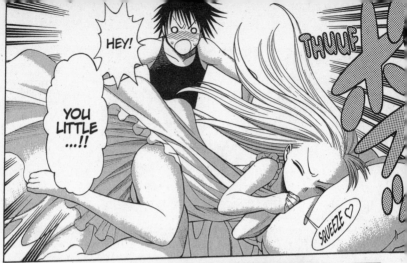

HEY!

THUNF

YOU LITTLE ...!!

SQUEEZE ♡

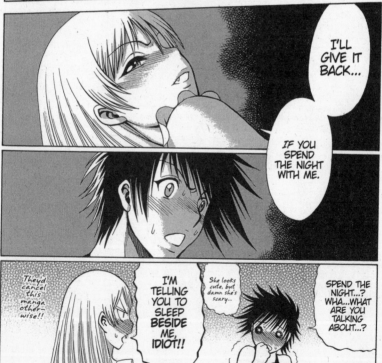

I'LL GIVE IT BACK...

IF YOU SPEND THE NIGHT WITH ME.

They'd cancel this manga otherwise!!

I'M TELLING YOU TO SLEEP BESIDE ME, IDIOT!!

She looks cute, but damn she's scary...

SPEND THE NIGHT...? WHA...WHAT ARE YOU TALKING ABOUT...?

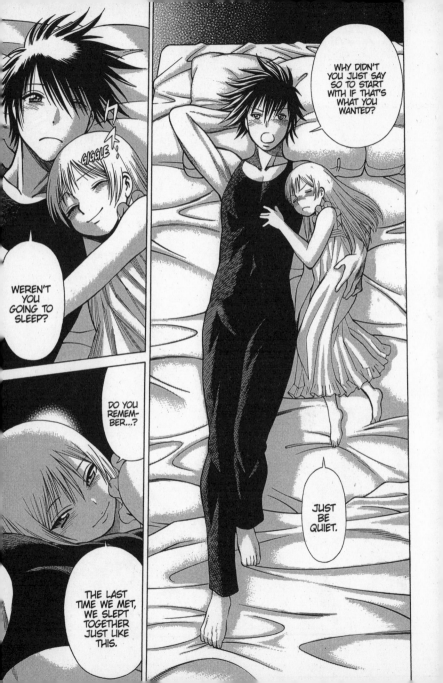

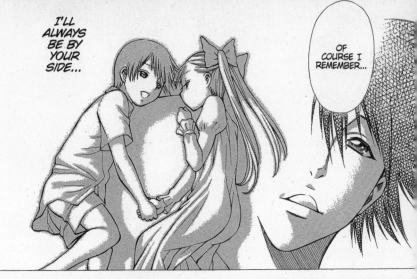

I'LL ALWAYS BE BY YOUR SIDE...

OF COURSE I REMEMBER...

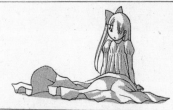

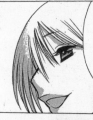

I WAS SAD WHEN I WOKE UP AND YOU WEREN'T THERE.

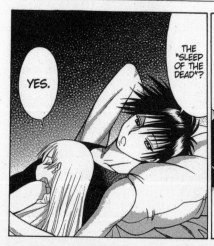

THE "SLEEP OF THE DEAD"?

YES.

I COULDN'T HELP IT! THAT'S HOW VAMPIRES SLEEP.

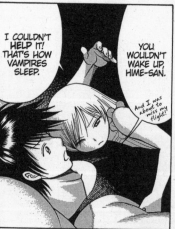

YOU WOULDN'T WAKE UP, HIME-SAN.

And I was about to miss my flight!

182

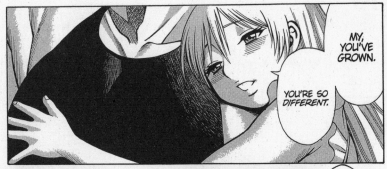

MY, YOU'VE GROWN.

YOU'RE SO DIFFERENT.

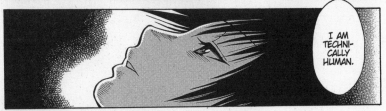

I AM TECHNI-CALLY HUMAN.

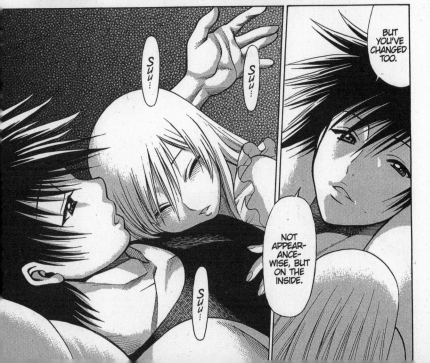

BUT YOU'VE CHANGED TOO.

SUU...

SUU...

NOT APPEAR-ANCE-WISE, BUT ON THE INSIDE.

SUU...

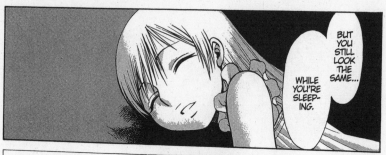

BUT YOU STILL LOOK THE SAME...

WHILE YOU'RE SLEEP-ING.

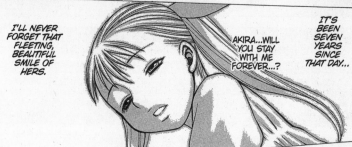

IT'S BEEN SEVEN YEARS SINCE THAT DAY...

AKIRA...WILL YOU STAY WITH ME FOREVER...?

I'LL NEVER FORGET THAT FLEETING, BEAUTIFUL SMILE OF HERS.

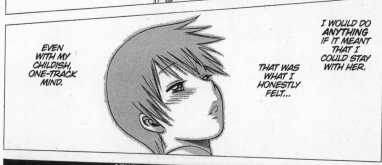

I WOULD DO ANYTHING IF IT MEANT THAT I COULD STAY WITH HER.

THAT WAS WHAT I HONESTLY FELT...

EVEN WITH MY CHILDISH, ONE-TRACK MIND.

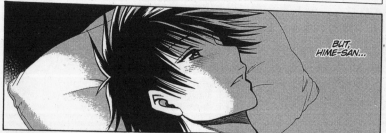

BUT, HIME-SAN...

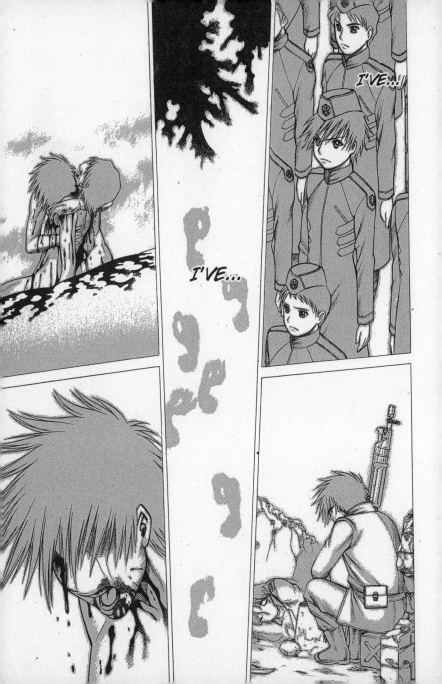

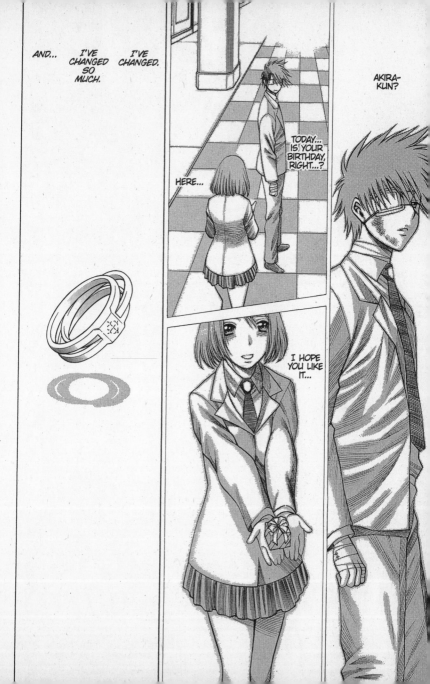

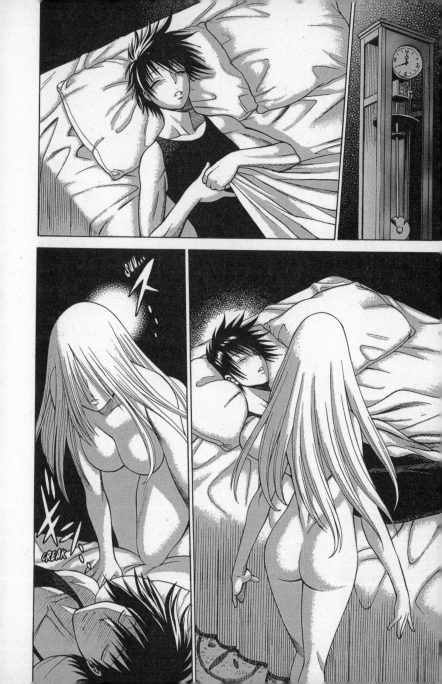

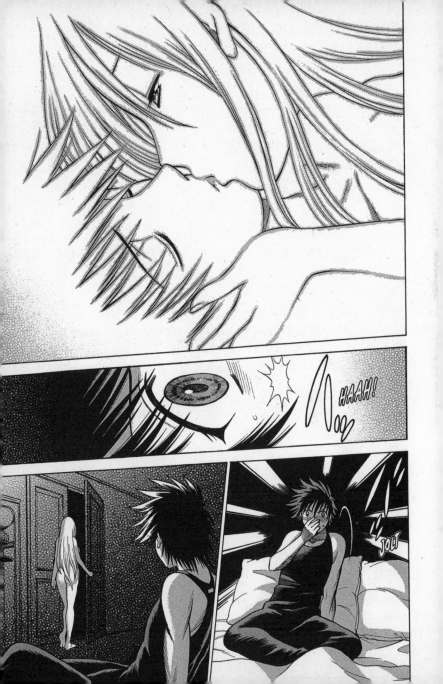

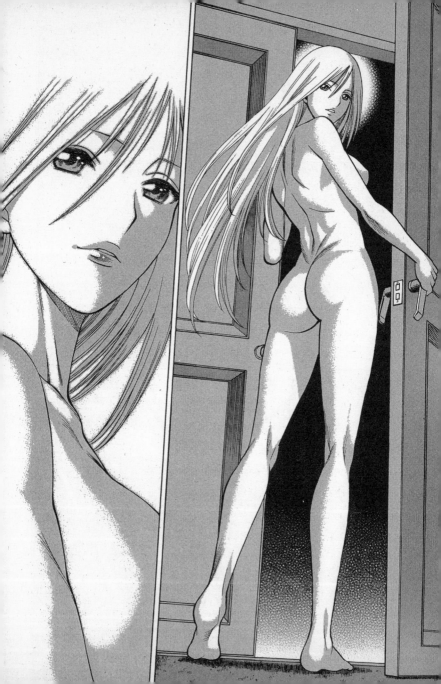

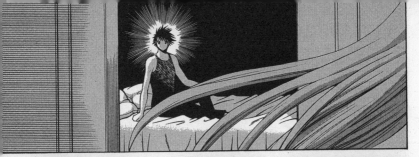

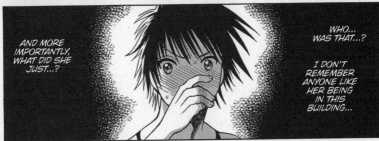

WHO... WAS THAT...?

I DON'T REMEMBER ANYONE LIKE HER BEING IN THIS BUILDING...

AND MORE IMPORTANTLY, WHAT DID SHE JUST...?

THERE WAS A WOMAN JUST--!

HEY, HIME-SAN, WAKE UP!

HIME ...?

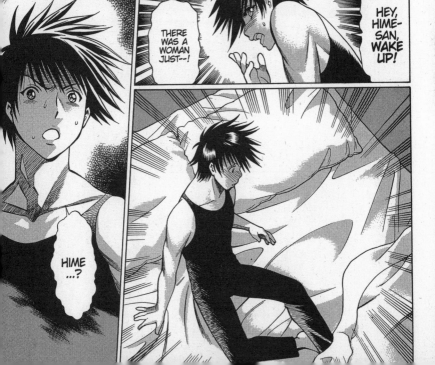

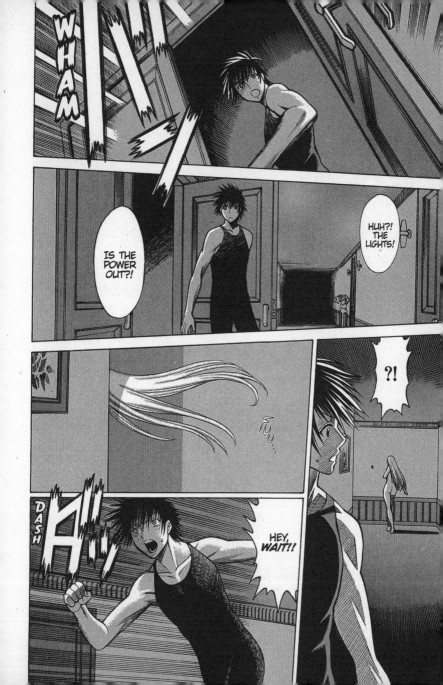

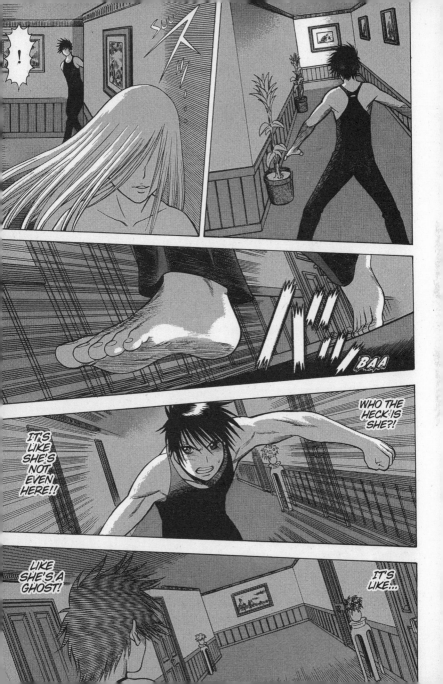

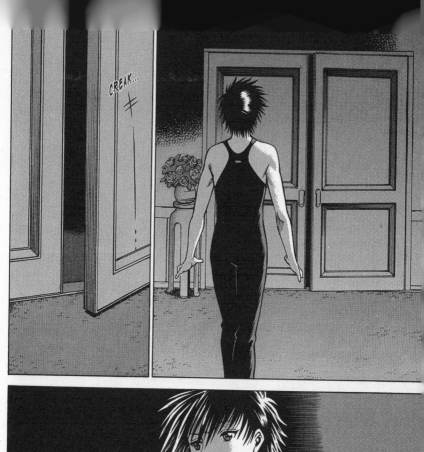

CREAK...

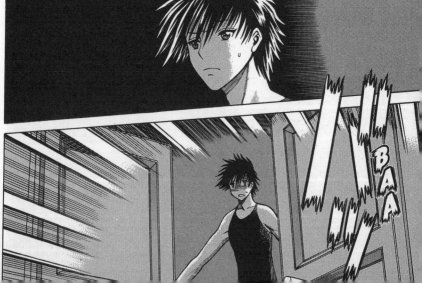

BAA

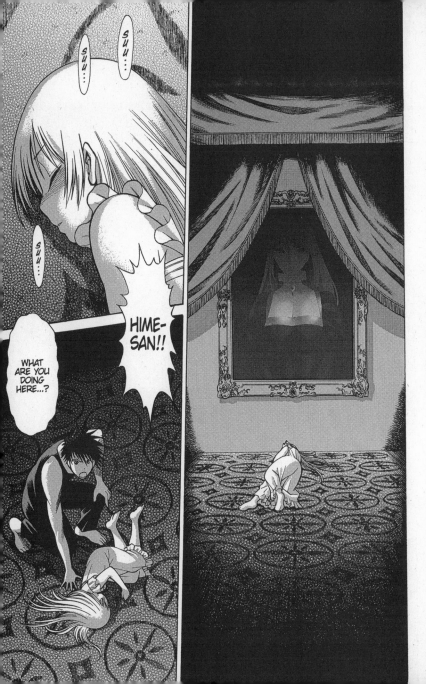

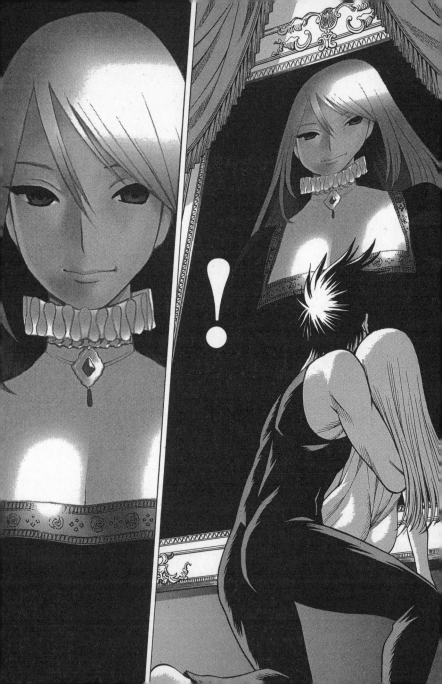

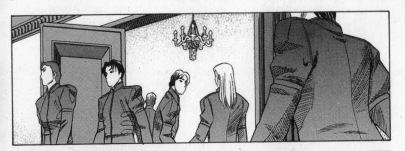

THERE'S NOTHING ON THE SECURITY CAMERAS ...?

AS FOR THE INTRUDER, WOLFGANG-DONO'S SEARCH OF THE MANOR HASN'T TURNED UP ANYTHING YET.

OH, HIME-SAMA...

DISAPPEARING FROM YOUR BEDROOM... WE WERE WORRIED ABOUT YOU.

UNFORTUNATELY, NO.

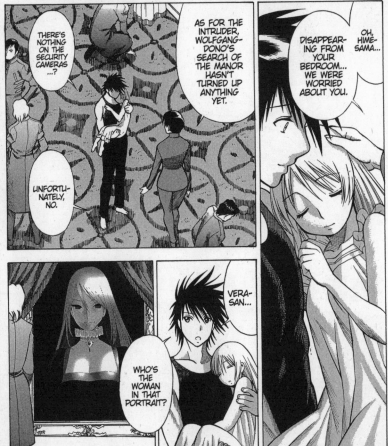

VERA-SAN...

WHO'S THE WOMAN IN THAT PORTRAIT?

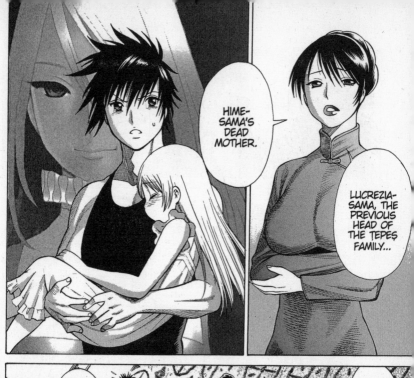

HIME-SAMA'S DEAD MOTHER.

LUCREZIA-SAMA, THE PREVIOUS HEAD OF THE TEPEŞ FAMILY...

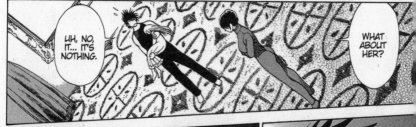

UH, NO, IT... IT'S NOTHING.

WHAT ABOUT HER?

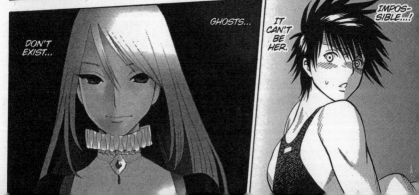

GHOSTS...

DON'T EXIST...

IT CAN'T BE HER.

IMPOS-SIBLE...!

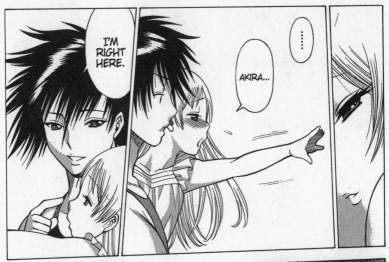

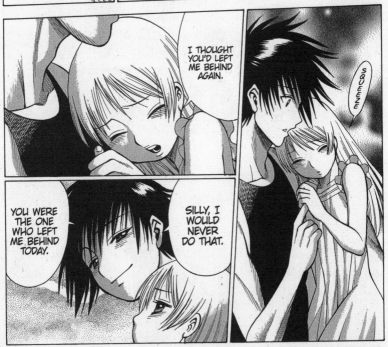

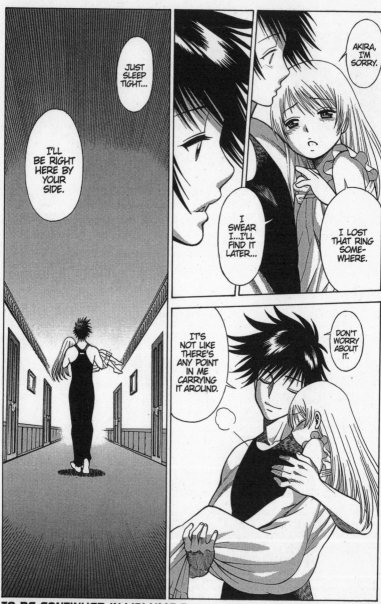

TO BE CONTINUED IN VOLUME 2

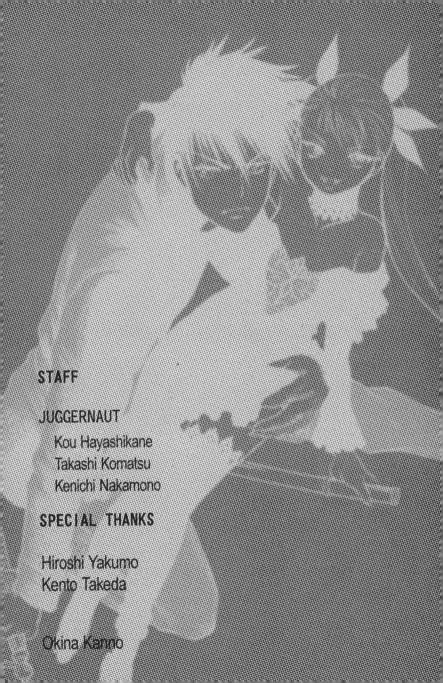

STAFF

JUGGERNAUT
Kou Hayashikane
Takashi Komatsu
Kenichi Nakamono

SPECIAL THANKS

Hiroshi Yakumo
Kento Takeda

Okina Kanno

Dance with the Vampire Maid

Book-only, freshly-penned 4-koma strips

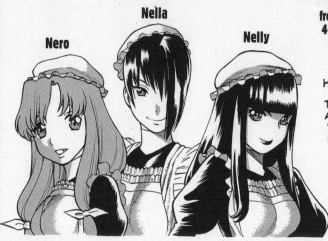

Nero

Nella

Nelly

HELLO THERE. WE'RE THE THREE MAIDS ASSIGNED TO SERVE MINA HIME-SAMA.

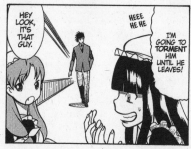

HEY LOOK, IT'S THAT GUY.

HEEE HE HE

I'M GOING TO TORMENT HIM UNTIL HE LEAVES!

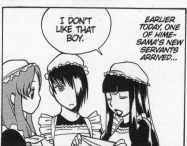

I DON'T LIKE THAT BOY.

EARLIER TODAY, ONE OF HIME-SAMA'S NEW SERVANTS ARRIVED...

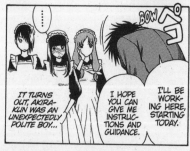

BOW ペこ

. . . . .

IT TURNS OUT, AKIRA-KUN WAS AN UNEXPECTEDLY POLITE BOY...

I HOPE YOU CAN GIVE ME INSTRUCTIONS AND GUIDANCE.

I'LL BE WORKING HERE, STARTING TODAY.

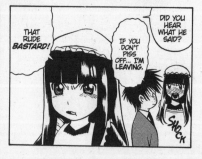

THAT RUDE *BASTARD!*

IF YOU DON'T PISS OFF... I'M LEAVING.

DID YOU HEAR WHAT HE SAID?

SHOCK

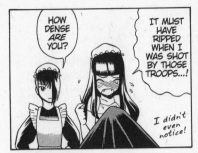

HOW DENSE ARE YOU?

IT MUST HAVE RIPPED WHEN I WAS SHOT BY THOSE TROOPS...!

I didn't even notice!

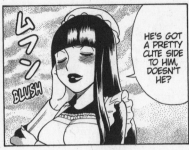

ムンン

BLUSH

HE'S GOT A PRETTY CUTE SIDE TO HIM, DOESN'T HE?

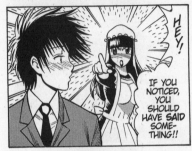

HEY!

IF YOU NOTICED, YOU SHOULD HAVE SAID SOMETHING!!

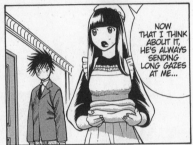

NOW THAT I THINK ABOUT IT, HE'S ALWAYS SENDING LONG GAZES AT ME...

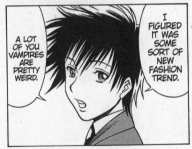

A LOT OF YOU VAMPIRES ARE PRETTY WEIRD.

I FIGURED IT WAS SOME SORT OF NEW FASHION TREND.

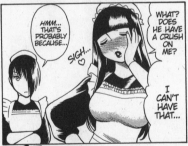

HMM... THAT'S PROBABLY BECAUSE...

SIGH...

WHAT? DOES HE HAVE A CRUSH ON ME?

I CAN'T HAVE THAT...

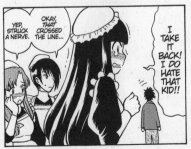

YEP, STRUCK A NERVE.

OKAY, THAT CROSSED THE LINE...

I TAKE IT BACK! I DO HATE THAT KID!!

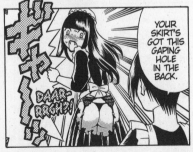

DAAR-RRGH!!

YOUR SKIRT'S GOT THIS GAPING HOLE IN THE BACK.

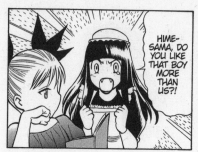

HIME-SAMA, DO YOU LIKE THAT BOY MORE THAN US?!

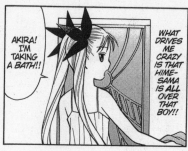

AKIRA! I'M TAKING A BATH!!

WHAT DRIVES ME CRAZY IS THAT HIME-SAMA IS ALL OVER THAT BOY!!

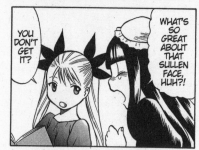

YOU DON'T GET IT?

WHAT'S SO GREAT ABOUT THAT SULLEN FACE, HUH?!

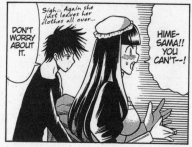

Sigh... Again she just leaves her clothes all over...

DON'T WORRY ABOUT IT.

HIME-SAMA!! YOU CAN'T--!

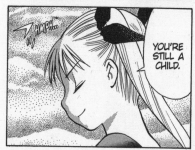

MMPH...

YOU'RE STILL A CHILD.

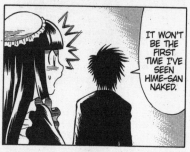

IT WON'T BE THE FIRST TIME I'VE SEEN HIME-SAN NAKED.

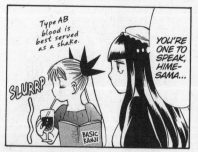

Type AB blood is best served as a shake.

SLURRP

BASIC KANJI

YOU'RE ONE TO SPEAK, HIME-SAMA...

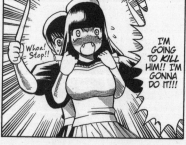

Whoa! Stop!!

I'M GOING TO KILL HIM!! I'M GONNA DO IT!!!

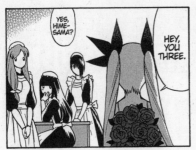

YES, HIME-SAMA?

HEY, YOU THREE.

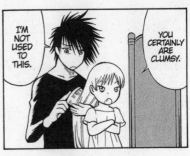

I'M NOT USED TO THIS.

YOU CERTAINLY ARE CLUMSY.

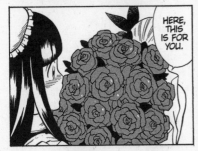

HERE, THIS IS FOR YOU.

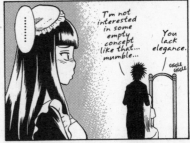

......

I'm not interested in some empty concept like that... mumble...

You lack elegance.

GIGGLE GIGGLE

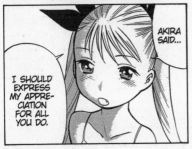

AKIRA SAID...

I SHOULD EXPRESS MY APPRECIATION FOR ALL YOU DO.

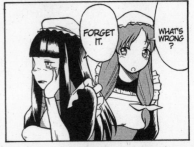

FORGET IT.

WHAT'S WRONG?

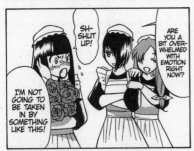

SH-SHUT UP!

ARE YOU A BIT OVERWHELMED WITH EMOTION RIGHT NOW?

I'M NOT GOING TO BE TAKEN IN BY SOMETHING LIKE THIS!

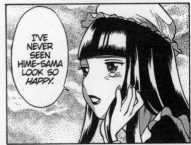

I'VE NEVER SEEN HIME-SAMA LOOK SO HAPPY.

CONTINUED TO VOLUME 2

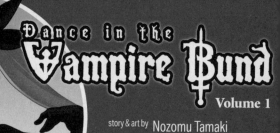

Dance in the Vampire Bund

Volume 1

story & art by Nozomu Tamaki

STAFF CREDITS

translation	**Kenji Komiya**
adaptation	**Katherine Bell, Adam Arnold**
retouch & lettering	**Aristotle Licuanan**
layout	**Bambi Eloriaga-Amago**
copy editor	**Lori Smith**
editor	**Adam Arnold**

publisher	**Seven Seas Entertainment**

DANCE IN THE VAMPIRE BUND VOL. 1
© 2006 by Nozomu Tamaki
First published in Japan in 2006 by MEDIA FACTORY, Inc.
English translation rights reserved by Seven Seas Entertainment, LLC.
Under the license from MEDIA FACTORY, Inc., Tokyo.

Visit us online at www.gomanga.com

ISBN: 978-1-933164-80-9

Printed in Canada

First printing: May 2008

10 9 8 7 6 5 4 3 2 1

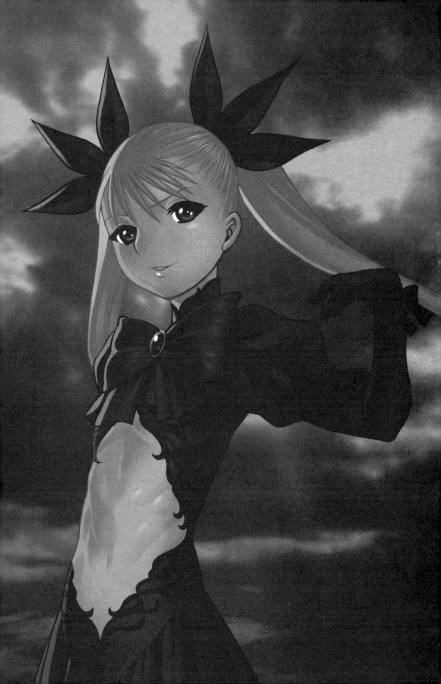

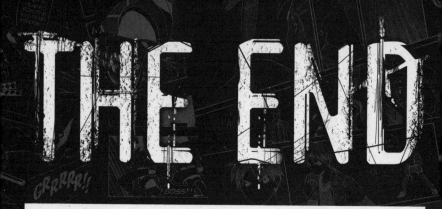

YOU'RE READING THE WRONG WAY

This is the last page of
Dance in the Vampire Bund
Volume 1.

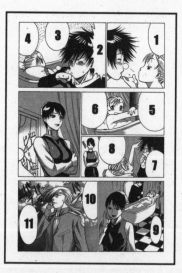

This book reads from right to left, Japanese style. To read from the beginning, flip the book over to the other side, start with the top right panel, and take it from there.

If this is your first time reading manga, just follow the diagram. It may seem backwards at first, but you'll get used to it! Have fun!